GOD'S PLEASURE AT WORK

BRIDGING THE SACRED-SECULAR DIVIDE

Real People — Real Faith — Real World

A Book-and-DVD curriculum that helps followers of Christ

to connect their work with "the faith given once for all" (Jude 3)

Dr. Christian Overman

Foreword and Afterword by John D. Beckett

To obtain the DVD
that accompanies this book,
call toll free 877.624.0230.

Responses to

GOD'S PLEASURE AT WORK

"The real-world models gave the course irrefutable credibility."

"Monday has more meaning now."

"I am more aware of the awesome opportunity that I have to fulfill God's purpose in my life through my work."

"If I had taken this course years ago, I'd still have my business."

"This is impacting my plans for employment."

"Revolutionary!"

GOD'S PLEASURE AT WORK

Bridging the Sacred-Secular Divide

Real People – Real Faith – Real World

A Book-and-DVD curriculum that helps followers of Christ
to connect their work with "the faith given once for all" (Jude 3)

ISBN: 978-0-9743425-2-8
Library of Congress Control Number: 2008944260

Most Scripture verses are from the New King James Version, copyright © 1982 , by Thomas Nelson, Inc.

Printed in the United States of America

Ablaze Publications
2800 122nd Place NE
Bellevue, Washington 98005-1520

*"To be sure, it's important for Christian scholars to conduct
research and hold academic symposia, but the real leverage for
cultural change comes from transforming the habits
and dispositions of ordinary people."*

Chuck Colson and Nancy Pearcey
How Now Shall We Live?

*"Jenny...I believe that God made me for a purpose. For China.
But He also made me fast. And when I run, I feel His pleasure.
To give it up would be to hold Him in contempt."*

Eric Liddell, Olympic runner
and missionary to China,
to his sister, Jenny,
in the film, *Chariots of Fire*

Table of Contents

Quick Start

God's Pleasure At Work: Bridging the Sacred-Secular Divide is a Book-and-DVD that helps followers of Christ to connect their work with their faith in winsome and practical ways. The text is to be read in conjunction with the viewing of over two dozen short DVD clips of real-world examples, supplemental content and helpful interviews.

Although this study may be done by individuals, the Book-and-DVD format was designed with small groups in mind. A small group may be a few friends meeting for *caffe lattes* on Saturday morning, a book club, a home-group on Tuesday nights, several employees getting together during the lunch break, or CEOs meeting early once a week before heading to the office. This course may also be done as an adult education elective at a local church or parish, or as part of a college business course, or a seminary class, or a career-orientation course in a Christian school.

If *God's Pleasure At Work* [GPAW] is being offered to a large group of people in a local church or parish, it is recommended that the group be divided into smaller discussion groups of about 4-8 people, with the same participants sitting together throughout the course. These sub-groups might be arranged with people sitting together who work in the same general fields, such as health service, education, sales, home-making, small business owners, or CEOs, but this arrangement is optional.

Group participants may read the text between meetings, or the text may be read aloud together when meeting. The viewing of the DVD is intended to be done when the group is together. Allow time for interaction, both with regard to what is read in the text and what is viewed on the DVD.

Avoid the tendency to feel you have to get through one chapter per week. Take whatever time is necessary to digest the material and to consider its full ramifications for the various participants in your group.

Those who find *God's Pleasure At Work: Bridging the Sacred-Secular Divide* helpful are encouraged to go on to the second book in the GPAW series, *God's Pleasure At Work: The Difference One Life Can Make.*

The DVD is vital to this curriculum. Many people who go through the course say the video examples of people who are integrating their faith with their work are the highlights of *God's Pleasure At Work*. There is no way written words alone can adequately communicate what many of these clips contain.

For many small groups, the viewing of the DVD may be accomplished through a laptop computer at the group meeting. Or, if the group is meeting in a home, the clips may be played on a television connected to a DVD player. For large groups, a video projector is recommended.

It is not expected that everyone in the group will have the DVD. Only the leader needs one. However, if any participants wish to have the DVD for home viewing, it is available through Worldview Matters by calling toll-free 877.624.0230.

God's Pleasure At Work is for anyone who works, whether as a CEO, a truck driver, or a stay-at-home mom. It applies to retired people, too, because "work" has very broad applications, and is not always something people do for pay.

May the Lord richly bless each of you, as you focus on aligning your faith with your work, whatever kind of work it may be!

The Worldview Matters Team
www.worldviewmatters.com

Preface and Acknowledgements

Occasionally I'm asked how *God's Pleasure At Work* came to be. The story begins back in 1979, when I was asked to take the role of principal in a Christian school in Seattle. To be better equipped, I enrolled in graduate level courses at Seattle Pacific University, where I pursued a Master of Education degree.

My studies included courses in philosophy of Christian education taught by Dr. Albert E. Greene, who helped me to understand the critical role that the biblical worldview plays in "thinking Christianly." For Dr. Greene's contribution to the basic content of the GPAW course, and for his example as a mentor and friend, I am especially grateful.

During the fourteen years I served as principal of a Christian school, I worked with classroom teachers on the art and science of making connections between academic subjects and the bigger picture of a biblical worldview that surrounds each subject taught in school.

During those years, I wrote a book on the topic of biblical worldview for my staff, parents and upper level students. That book, published by Tyndale House in 1989, titled, *Different Windows*, now goes by the title *Assumptions That Affect Our Lives*, and is published by Ablaze Publishing.

As time went by, a training workshop, called, *Think Again!*, was developed to go with the *Assumptions* text. This workshop was put into DVD format, and was approved by the Association of Christian Schools International as a Continuing Education course in Biblical Studies. The *Think Again!* DVD curriculum has been used around the world by Christian schools as a staff in-service training tool, and by homeschooling families and church groups as a basic course in "worldview."

An additional course specifically for teachers, on designing lesson plans that integrate biblical worldview into all academic subjects, called, *Making the Connections,* was developed through my long association with Don Johnson and Cascade Christian Schools, in Puyallup, Washington. Over the years, I have had the privilege of teaching *Think Again!* and *Making the Connections* to groups throughout the United States and in Central America, Europe, Africa and Asia.

In 2004, I enrolled in the Doctor of Ministry program at Bakke Graduate University, focusing on theology of work. Here I was influenced by the thinking of Ray Bakke, Dennis Bakke and Lowell Bakke. My doctoral project became the *God's Pleasure At Work* curriculum.

Then in 2008, I was privileged to participate in Chuck Colson's Centurion Program. This intensive, one-year program equips followers of Christ "to think Christianly in order to apply biblical truth to all of life and to engage and shape the culture out of a biblical framework." It was during this experience that I was inspired to put GPAW into the current Book-and-DVD format, to "reach the masses." I am eternally grateful to Chuck Colson for the enormous encouragement he has been to me personally since 2001.

For help in understanding biblical worldview in general, I am indebted to numerous writers and educators, such as Francis Schaeffer, James Sire, Albert Wolters, Charles Colson, Nancy Pearcey, Marvin Olasky, Herbert Schlossberg, Harry Blamires, Ronald Nash, David Noebel, Frank Gaebeline, H. W. Byrne, William Brown, Gary Phillips, Timothy Evearitt and Albert E. Greene, Jr.

For help in understanding how biblical worldview relates to work, I am indebted to Stephen Graves, Thomas Addington, Paul Stevens, Doug Sherman, William Hendricks, Ken Eldred, Os Hillman, Max DePree, Don Flow, Darrow Miller, Dennis Peacocke and Michael Baer.

I also want to thank those who contributed greatly via video or phone interviews: John Beckett, Jack vanHartesvelt, Gary Starkweather, Al Erisman (who also recommended I put GPAW into book form), Lowell Bakke, Bonnie Wurzbacher, Aila Tasse, Nancy Pearcey, Phil Cooke, Paul Stevens, David Carlson and Chuck Colson.

I'm also grateful to Katie Sisco for her superb editing and proofreading, and to Ron Imhoff and Glenn Bond for reviewing the manuscript and providing many suggestions that made this a better book.

Finally, words cannot express my gratitude to my extraordinary wife, Kathy, who since 1970 has been my constant help and vital friend. Thanks, m'Love.

Christian Overman
Founding Director
Worldview Matters

Foreword

I had been leading a rapidly growing manufacturing business for over 15 years when a friend gave me Christian Overman's first book, then titled *Different Windows* (now titled, *Assumptions That Affect Our Lives*). As an engineer by training, I remember thinking, "I don't know that I can wade through all this stuff about Greek philosophy and its impact on culture."

By this time, however, I had become serious about applying biblical Christianity to my work. Maybe this book could help. And frankly, I wanted to respect the counsel of my friend: "John, you really want to read Overman's book. It's great!"

Am I ever glad I did. To say *Different Windows* revolutionized my thinking would be an understatement. As I finished it—the well worn pages now replete with underlining and marginal notes—I thought, "if I weren't a proper Episcopalian I'd be doing cartwheels right now!"

Simply, yet profoundly, Christian unpacked for me the radical difference between the way Greeks viewed the world—beginning a thousand years before Christ—and the Hebraic (biblical) worldview. This wasn't a stuffy history lesson. It was both relevant and practical. It demolished the subtle yet pervasive idea that my involvement in business should be viewed through both secular and sacred lenses. God didn't intend that I would be one person on Sunday, another on Monday.

Later, I found Overman was in good company, as I began gleaning from such towering worldview thinkers as Abraham Kuyper, Francis Schaeffer and A.W. Tozer. Tozer, in particular, struck a vital chord when he wrote in *The Pursuit of God:*

> *One of the greatest hindrances to the Christian's internal peace is the common habit of dividing our lives into two areas — the sacred and the secular. But this state of affairs is totally unnecessary. We have gotten ourselves on the horns of a dilemma, but the dilemma is not real. It is the creature of misunderstanding. The secular-sacred antithesis has no foundation in the New Testament.*

I have wondered, "could I have been a business success without the help Overman provided in my understanding of worldview?" Perhaps so. But meeting business challenges without this perspective would have been like going into a boxing ring with one arm tied behind my back. I believe I might still share the nagging struggle I see with so many folks in the marketplace—viewing my daily work as secondary to my "real life" as a believer.

Christian could easily have stopped his pursuits after writing his first book. If he had, we would still be better for his initial exposition on worldview. But to our great benefit he continued to develop, refine and repackage the message. I am particularly grateful that in *God's Pleasure At Work* he has targeted the workplace. For too long, those of us in business have behaved as though our work falls outside God's interest or involvement.

Now, because Christian took the next step, you have in your hands the finest and most practically helpful publication ever produced on this subject. I truly believe the marketplace, and all it touches worldwide, will be propelled into closer alignment with our God and His purposes—and will be enormously more fruitful—as we lay hold of these timeless truths.

So fasten your seatbelt. Be prepared to challenge "traditional" thinking. Learn to see the world as God sees it. Then watch for the explosion of His favor in your life and work in ways you never imagined.

John D. Beckett
Chairman, The Beckett Companies
Elyria, Ohio
Author, Loving Monday *(www.lovingmonday.com)*
and Mastering Monday *(www.masteringmonday.com)*

Chapter One

Why Worldview Matters

DVD Clip #1
Welcome by Chuck Colson
Approx. 1 minute

Welcome to *God's Pleasure At Work*! I'm so glad you've taken this step. I trust that by the time we're finished, you'll be glad too.

Although the GPAW study can be done by individuals, there are advantages in participating with a small group, where you can discuss practical applications and build supportive relationships. Increased learning will take place this way, particularly if your group shares a common occupational affinity, such as a group of health care workers, or CEOs, homemakers, or educators.

If finding an "affinity group" is not possible, any group that will provide stimulating conversation will help. You might want to go through this course with just one other person, such as a close friend, a co-worker, a spouse, or a teenage son or daughter.

Plan to meet once a week to discuss what you have read and to view the DVD together. The DVD is a vital part of GPAW. "Talking Points" are included in the text, to provide focus points for discussion and application, but feel free to create your own Talking Points.

OK. Let's get started!

BRING MEANING TO OUR WORK

To really know and experience God's pleasure at work, we must understand God's *reasons* for work. To really understand how work can be as significant for the plumber as it is for the pastor, it helps to understand *why work* — all kinds of work — *is truly significant to God.*

A familiar parable is worth repeating here. It illustrates the profound truth that we don't *get* meaning *from* our work, we *bring* meaning *to* our work. The story goes like this: Three men were laying bricks. When the first man was asked what he was doing, he replied, "I'm laying bricks." When the second man was asked, he said, "I'm building a wall." But the third man declared, "I'm building a cathedral!"

Bonnie Wurzbacher is the Senior Vice President of Global Accounts for The Coca-Cola Company. In a phone conversation with Bonnie, she reminded me of the story of the three bricklayers. She then went on to tell me about what *she* needed to know before she could truly see how her work fulfills and advances God's purposes for the world. When you get together with your group, listen to what Bonnie shared with me by viewing DVD clip #2.

DVD Clip #2
Bonnie Wurzbacher on Bringing Meaning to Work
Approx. 1 minute

Seeing how a *pastor's* work "fulfills and advances God's purposes for the world" is one thing, but seeing how a *corporate executive's* work fulfills and advances God's purposes for the world is quite another!

Exactly what kind of "theology of work" allowed Bonnie Wurzbacher, a business executive, to see her work as *fulfilling and advancing the purposes of God for the world?* And how did she come to embrace a worldview that says *"there is no secular and sacred split?"*

We'll understand more about what Bonnie meant by the "secular-sacred split" as we go along. But first, let's examine some faulty assumptions about reality that have had a profound effect on the way most Christians think about work.

Examining assumptions is important, because this is where decisions *start*, and actions *germinate*. All of our actions, including our actions at work, are guided by deeply held beliefs and assumptions that we rarely examine or bring to the surface. Yet, these deeply held beliefs subconsciously guide our everyday behavior at work.

Talking Point: Can you think of examples of workplace behavior that is shaped by beliefs or assumptions rarely discussed or examined?

When your small group gets together this week, you'll participate in a short memory exercise. First, you will be asked to memorize a picture. When you view this picture on DVD clip #3, try to remember as many details as you can. Allow every detail to be burned into your memory.

Near the end of DVD clip #3, a particular part of the picture will be circled. This is an important part of the memory exercise. You will understand why later. For now, just try to memorize the picture.

DVD Clip #3
Visual Memory Exercise
Approx. 1 minute

We'll come back to the memory exercise later, but first, let's talk a bit about workplace *values* and *behavior*.

On the next page, you'll see three concentric circles. Write the word "behavior" at the bottom of the outer circle.

Behavior is what is *said* or *done*, and it's also what is *not* said, and what is *not* done. In the context of the workplace, the behavior of an auto mechanic revolves around such things as repairing what's broken, servicing moving parts, analyzing engine problems, ordering supplies, learning new automotive skills and communicating with the boss, with co-workers and with customers.

The behavior of homemakers revolves around things like conflict resolution, money management, taxi service, child education, nutritional science and organizational management. CEO behavior has to do with things like contracts, marketing, salary and benefits issues, public relations, hiring and firing, government regulations and profit distribution. In the business world, it's the company's "Strategic Plan" and "Procedure Manual" that deals with matters at the behavior level.

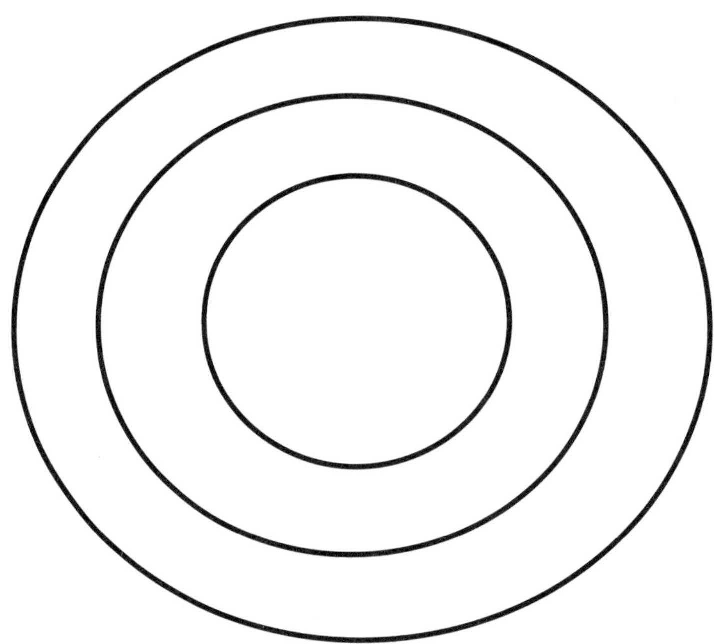

But the big question is, *what drives or guides behavior?*

To get to the "driver-guider" behind behavior, we have to go deeper than the behaviors themselves. Most people who want to see good practice in the workplace agree that *values* drive behavior. So let's write the word "values" in the second circle, directly above the word "behavior."

For some workers, the value of a weekly paycheck keeps them behaving certain ways on the job. But most companies don't want the value of a paycheck to be the most important value governing workplace behavior. That's why many companies and organizations hang their "Core Values" in a nice frame on the lobby wall.

What are some typical values in the workplace? They include excellence, integrity, leadership, justice, respect, trust, friendliness and truthfulness. Many companies and organizations have a formal document called "Guiding Principles," and virtually all companies have a

"Mission Statement." These documents explain to employees and executives alike what the company highly values, and these documents provide a platform upon which the company's Strategic Plan and Procedure Manual rest — at least in theory.

But values don't come out of a vacuum! Behind values is something even more basic. Something that answers the *"What for?"* questions. It's one thing for an organization or a company to identify "excellence" as a core value, but it's quite another thing to determine *why* excellence is a core value. Is it just so that more sales will be made, or is there more to it?

When we push the "why" question back as far as we can go, we eventually arrive at *worldview* beliefs. So let's write the word "worldview" in the center circle.

Here's the key thought so far: *A person's values and attitude flow out of his or her worldview.*

For followers of Christ who want to fulfill and advance the purposes of God for the world, and who want to align their workplace behavior with God's purposes for work, it's critical to look *beyond values* to a deeper level, to the specific biblical worldview premises that shape and govern those values.

Identifying specific biblical premises and then discovering how these truths can generate workplace values and behavior is what *God's Pleasure At Work* is all about. A biblically-informed worldview provides meaning and "staying power" for workplace values and behavior, and this is why worldview matters!

When Bonnie Wurzbacher understood the ramifications of the biblical worldview for her daily work at Coca Cola, and realized there is no "sacred and secular split," she recognized how her work actually fulfills and advances God's purposes for the world. This epiphany occurred because her *"what for?"* questions were answered.

To get to the heart of what all this really means, let's define the word "worldview" and give examples of how a worldview shapes the values that influence human behavior — whether one is on the job or off.

DEFINING WORLDVIEW

A simple definition of worldview is: *"A comprehensive framework of beliefs that helps us to interpret what we see and experience and also gives us direction in the choices that we make as we live out our days."* (Richard Wright, Professor, Gordon College.)

Christianity is a worldview. And so is Buddhism. So are Hinduism and Humanism. Each of these worldviews, as with all other worldviews, answer five basic questions about what is truly real:

1. *Who or what is the ultimate authority or highest power, and what is the nature and role of this force or entity?*
2. *What makes up all the stuff of the universe, how did it get here, and is there more to it than meets the eye?*
3. *Who are human beings, what gives them value, what happens when they die, and how do they know what is true?*
4. *How do people determine right and wrong?*
5. *Is there a reason and purpose for all that exists?*

Whatever people believe (or assume) with respect to these five critical questions will determine their worldview, which will shape their values and influence their behavior.

Talking Point: Which of the five basic worldview questions given above do you think plays the most important role in shaping the values and behavior of people in *your* particular line of work? Why?

Behavior is often a focus in the media. Values are sometimes discussed, but worldview assumptions are rarely mentioned. Yet, everyone has a worldview, even if they're not able to recognize it or articulate it for others.

God's Pleasure At Work is about recognizing biblical worldview premises that specifically relate to work (your work in particular), and then aligning those premises with workplace values and behavior that can ultimately renew the community and transform culture.

But before we get to these premises, let's talk a bit about faulty premises that have had debilitating effects upon followers of Christ in the workplace when it comes to seeing how the work of a plumber really fulfills and advances God's purposes for the world.

Faulty assumptions can have hazardous consequences. The Bible says that one consequence of faulty assumptions is that we can be "taken captive." Why such strong language? According to Scripture, followers of Christ are in a heated spiritual battle with serious consequences.

When the apostle Paul cautioned followers of Christ in the city of Colosse about this spiritual battle, he wrote: *"See to it that no one takes you captive through philosophy and empty deception according to the traditions of men and not according to Christ…"* (Colossians 2:8)

Paul was not saying that all philosophy is bad. The word "philosophy" simply means "love of wisdom" in the Greek language. Loving wisdom is a good thing. But philosophy that is *"not according to Christ"* is a problem.

Paul was not saying "don't think!" He was saying just the opposite. He was telling the Colossians to think carefully, and to make sure their thinking was aligned with a philosophy that was "according to Christ."

Paul didn't want the early Christians to be passive when it came to thinking skills. Indeed, he wanted them to be active thinkers. In II Corinthians 10:5, Paul exhorted the followers of Christ in Corinth to *"take every thought captive to the obedience of Christ."* (II Corinthians 10:5) This is not an easy thing to do. But it is vitally important.

In athletic terms, Colossians 2:8 is a *defensive* skill and II Corinthians 10:5 is an *offensive* skill. To win, we need both.

In these passages, Paul presents two alternatives with respect to our thoughts: We can either be *taken captive by thoughts* according to the traditions of men, or we can *take thoughts captive* to the obedience of Christ. I don't know about you, but I'd rather *take* thoughts captive than *be taken* captive *by* thoughts.

But this raises the all-important question, *how* do we take thoughts captive to the obedience of Christ *in the workplace?* What does this really mean in the context of our daily work?

I am convinced that taking thoughts captive to the obedience of Christ is a learned skill. And because of this conviction, we'll be examining some practical tools for taking thoughts captive to the obedience of Christ in the context of your occupation.

The first step in taking thoughts captive to the obedience of Christ is to fully understand that whether we're *taken* captive by thoughts or we *take* thoughts captive depends upon one critical factor: our *worldview.*

When you get together with your small group this week, you will be shown a small part of a larger picture. This small part will appear in DVD clip #4. Most of the larger picture will be blacked out. Your task is to figure out what the meaning of the picture is, even though you can only see a small part of the whole. Try to identify what you are seeing, and describe the fuller, complete picture with as much detail as you can.

DVD Clip #4
The Function of a Larger Frame of Reference
Approx. 1.5 minute

This simple exercise illustrates the fact that people interpret smaller things in light of larger wholes. As seen in DVD clip #4, the meaning that people give to the smaller piece that appears on the screen is determined by the larger image which is resident within the mind from the earlier memory exercise. Because of this "resident image," or "larger mental frame of reference," meaning and understanding is attached, to the point of many details.

This is what a worldview does. It provides a larger mental "frame of reference" that causes us to interpret "smaller pieces" in certain ways, and to bring meaning to those smaller pieces. This is why it is critically important to have an image of the "bigger picture" in mind that provides the necessary frame of reference to make proper sense of the "smaller pieces."

The "smaller pieces" of life include all the issues and activities we deal with in the workplace, where most of us spend about one-third of our adult lives. How we see our co-workers and customers, and how we view our products, and our purpose, will be profoundly affected by our mental concept of the bigger picture of reality which is resident within our minds: our *worldview*.

Talking Point: What will be your primary "take-away" from this chapter?

Chapter Two
How Worldview Shapes Culture

Like our lives, every building is constructed on a set of beliefs and assumptions. To the untrained eye, a structure may appear perfect on the outside. But drill down into the framework and you'll discover what a building is truly made of.

If a builder makes faulty assumptions at the foundation level, any building may be compromised. Perhaps the effects won't be immediately visible, but over time—perhaps in a year, five years, or maybe ten—faulty assumptions will eventually become evident. But if the builder makes solid choices grounded in reliable building standards, a structure can stand the test of time.

In the same way, the biblical worldview provides a foundation for Christ's followers in the workplace. When that worldview is grounded on God's standards, it provides long-term strength and lasting stability. Call it "staying power."

In Chapter 1, we established why a person's worldview matters. In this chapter we'll examine five critical pillars upon which a biblically based worldview is constructed.

A working definition of worldview that incorporates the five pillars I'm referring to goes like this: *A worldview is a "big picture" of reality shaped by conscious beliefs or sub-conscious assumptions about God, Creation, Humanity, Moral Order and Purpose.*

We'll briefly examine these five worldview pillars one at a time, and see why each of them plays a critical role in determining the values that influence personal behavior and workplace values, and ultimately shapes the culture of communities as well as nations.

First of all, a person's beliefs or assumptions about *God* will be revealed in how they answer this question: *"Who or what is the ultimate authority or highest power, and what is the nature and role of this force or entity?"*

Even people holding to atheistic worldviews (such as Marxist Leninism or Humanism) have beliefs about God. They believe that He does not exist! Whether atheists admit it or not, this is a *faith* position. It's my opinion that it takes more faith to believe God *doesn't* exist, than to believe that He *does!*

If your big picture of ultimate reality tells you there is no personal, transcendent God to whom you are responsible and accountable, this belief will have a profound effect on your values and behavior in the workplace—and everywhere else.

Talking Point: Can you give some examples of how a belief in "no God" can affect behavior in the workplace?

Secondly, all worldviews are shaped by beliefs or assumptions about *Creation*. When I use the word "Creation," I'm referring to that which is "really real," in time and space. This worldview component corresponds to the question, *"What makes up all the stuff of the universe, how did it get here, and is there more to it than meets the eye?"*

"Creation" has to do with the question of what's really real with respect to the material and spiritual aspects of life. Some worldviews hold to the belief that all that's really real is *matter*. Period. Nothing else exists. There is no spiritual dimension in the universe. If you hold to this belief, it will have a profound effect upon both your values and behavior in the workplace. Other worldviews hold that matter is an illusion.

Some worldviews hold to the idea that there's more to reality than we can touch, taste, see, smell, hear or measure. There is a spiritual dimension that is every bit as real as the material dimension. Christianity is such a worldview, and this view can have a profound effect upon a person's values and behavior at work, as we'll see throughout this study.

The third pillar that holds up all worldviews is one's view of *Humanity*. This worldview component has to do with what we believe to be true about human beings. It corresponds to this question: *"Who are human beings, what gives them value, what happens when they die, and how do they know what is true?"*

What we believe about the nature, value and destiny of all human beings will greatly affect how we relate to co-workers, customers, and clients.

For followers of Christ who assume that biblical revelation is *universally* true (that is, true for all people, regardless of their personal feelings about it), then what the Scripture says about the nature, worth and destiny of human beings should have a major value-shaping effect on Christians in the workplace. For example, a worker who truly believes that all human beings are made in the likeness and image of God, as the Bible asserts, will treat co-workers and clients with profound respect at all times and in all circumstances, regardless of color or creed.

The fourth pillar that provides a foundation for all worldviews is the *Moral Order* component. This component corresponds to the question, *"How do people determine right and wrong?"* Is morality pre-determined by a higher authority (such as God), or is it something people just determine for themselves? Again, the answer to this question has enormous ramifications for the workplace.

The fifth and final pillar of all worldviews is *Purpose*. This component corresponds to the question, *"Is there a reason and purpose for all that exists?"* Christianity has some very compelling things to say about purpose, particularly with respect to work, as we'll see later.

Talking Point: Can you name one particular Christian belief about *purpose* that relates to *your* work?

The big challenge we have as followers of Christ is to consistently keep the "big picture" in mind as we consider the "smaller pieces" of life — particularly those everyday things that we encounter at work.

If we look at the issues and events of our work-life in isolation, that is, *disconnected* from the larger frame-of-reference (our worldview), we'll tend to focus on the "smaller pieces" and not take into consideration how those smaller piece fit into the larger whole. And when we view things out of context like this, we won't see things as they *really* are. We may be seeing a foothill at sunset, when in reality it is a banana.

TWO EXAMPLES

When the big picture is off-base, it's easy to misinterpret the smaller pieces. Let me give you two real-life examples of how the bigger picture of a worldview affects the way people interpret life. We'll look at an Eastern example first, and then a Western example.

According to the Hindu big picture, or the Hindu worldview, the idea of "karma" and "reincarnation" go hand-in-glove. If you do bad things in this life (like stealing or being cruel to others) your karma will dictate that you pay for your bad deeds in your next life. In other words, you must suffer in your reincarnated life for the suffering you caused in this life. What this tells you, if you're consistent with your worldview, is that people in poverty and suffering are in that condition *because their karma requires it.* They *have* to suffer for what they did in their previous life. It is their *duty!*

With this in mind, it would not be a good thing to relieve the suffering of people in poverty. After all, they are in that condition for a reason. They deserve it. Relieving their condition would do such people a great disservice, because in the next life they will have to return once again to a condition of poverty and pain because you messed with their karma. Such a worldview has had huge ramifications for India.

Talking Point: If anyone in your group has lived in India, share some examples of how the Hindu worldview has affected Indian attitudes and practices related to work and to occupations.

The West has its own culture-shaping worldviews with big ramifications for society. Take the worldview of Humanism, for example. Some people refer to it as "Secular Humanism," but I just call it "Humanism," because there is really only one kind of Humanism, and that is the kind which leaves God out of the picture. Some Humanists refer to Humanism as "Religious Humanism." Yes, it is "religious," but it is a religion without God. It is a well-defined, atheistic worldview. It is a rather young one, as far as established worldviews go, having only been formalized in the 20th Century. The first Humanist Manifesto was written in 1933. A second Manifesto came out in 1973, and a third in the year 2000.

If you do an Internet search of "Humanist Manifesto" you will find links to the texts of these manifests. I suggest you read them before you get together with your small group. Each Manifesto is short. After reading them, ask yourself: What is *in harmony* here with the biblical worldview, and what is *in conflict* with the biblical worldview?

Below are five statements taken from Humanist Manifestos I, II and III, with one statement corresponding to each of the five worldview pillars of God, Creation, Humanity, Moral Order and Purpose:

1. GOD: *We find insufficient evidence for belief in the existence of the supernatural; as non-theists, we begin with humans, not God, nature, not deity.*
2. CREATION: *The universe is self-existing and not created.*
3. HUMANITY: *Humans are an integral part of nature, the result of unguided evolutionary change.*
4. MORAL ORDER: *Moral values derive their source from human experience. Ethics is autonomous and situational.*
5. PURPOSE: *We can discover no divine purpose or providence for the human species...humans are responsible for what we are or will become. No deity will save us; we must save ourselves.*

Talking Point: How might the following enterprises be viewed differently by a Humanist than by a follower of Christ, and *why*? a) Providing "adult" entertainment, b) Operating a Christian school, c) Running an abortion clinic.

TREE ENCOUNTERS

The big picture of a worldview causes people to see and interpret many "smaller things" of life in different ways. The big picture may even cause people to view trees quite differently.

When your small group meets this week, you will watch a short DVD clip of a group of people viewing and interacting with trees in a way that reflects a different "big picture" of reality than most followers of Christ adhere to. As your group watches this clip, think about what specific view of God, Creation, Humanity, Moral Order or Purpose might possibly lie behind the values and behaviors of the people you will see.

Be organized and sequential about your analysis of what you see and hear. Specifically, after you view the clip, begin by discussing how the "God factor" guides these people's interaction with trees, and then how the "Creation factor" does so, then how the "Humanity," "Moral Order" and "Purpose" factors affect their interaction with trees.

One big caution: All non-biblical worldviews contain some elements of truth. It might be easy to view this DVD clip and only focus on elements that are in conflict with the biblical worldview, and miss elements that are *in harmony with* the biblical worldview. For this reason, begin your discussion with some observations about what is *congruent* with the biblical view *before* you talk about what is *not.*

This video clip is not shown in order to be critical of anyone. The people in the video are making an honest effort to live in alignment with their worldview, and this is a major step in anyone's life. The purpose of watching the video is to illustrate the connections between one's worldview and one's values or behavior.

DVD Clip #5
American Animism
Approx. 1 minute

Talking Point: What did you see in this video that was *congruent* with the biblical worldview? What was *not* congruent with the biblical worldview?

A *biblically informed* worldview affects not only the way people view trees and rocks, but the way people view their work. For followers of Christ, the biblical "big picture of reality" can guide them in the decisions they make as they seek to align their worldview with their work in a way that is intentional, winsome and authentic. Behind this goal is the central premise that worldview shapes values, values influence behavior, and the collective behaviors of various groups of people create culture.

One day, I shared this premise with someone who replied, "But doesn't it work the other way around? Doesn't culture influence people's behavior, shape their values and determine their worldview?"

Well, actually, for most people it *does* work that way.

But for followers of Christ the process is to be reversed. Romans 12:2 says, "*And do not be conformed to this world-system* [the Phillips translation says: 'Don't let the world around you squeeze you into its own mold'], *but be transformed by the renewing of your mind* [Phillips says, 'let God re-mold your minds from within'], *that you may prove what is that good and acceptable and perfect will of God.*"

Talking Point: What kinds of specific pressures at work try to "squeeze you into the mold of the world around you?"

When we have a "renewed mind," as Paul put it, we can be *intentional* about aligning our work with a biblical worldview. We can be *deliberate* about figuring out how to align our workplace values and behavior with core beliefs that are biblically informed. What better place to prove the good, acceptable and perfect will of God than in the workplace, where many of us spend about half of our waking hours?

We're going to look at some examples of companies whose cultures have been intentionally shaped by people who are living out the implications of their biblical faith in the context of their work.

One such person is John Beckett, Chairman of The Beckett Companies, in Elyria, Ohio. In Chapter 5, we'll take a close look at John Beckett and the effects that his biblical worldview has had on the culture of his company. But first, I'd like you and your small group to view an edited one-minute segment of a longer feature story that ABC News did on John Beckett in 1995. (You'll see the full story in Chapter 5.) As you view this short preview, watch for at least *four* specific biblical worldview beliefs John Beckett holds which have shaped the culture of The Beckett Companies.

Note John Beckett's intentionality in making deliberate alignments between his faith and his work.

DVD Clip #6
Shaping the Culture of a Company
Approx. 1 minute

Talking Point: What specific biblical beliefs can you identify from DVD clip #6 that shape the culture of The Beckett Companies?

The wonderful thing is, we don't have to be the CEO to align biblical beliefs with our work. *Any* participant in the workplace, from the line worker to the president, can align biblical premises with the work that is within one's own spheres of responsibility and influence, no matter how large or small.

The objectives of the GPAW course are threefold: a) to bring biblical worldview premises to the surface where they can be intentionally examined, b) to determine specific workplace values that might stem from those premises, and c) to consider workplace behaviors that might flow from those values.

The ultimate goals of the GPAW course are also threefold: a) to invigorate the workplace, b) to renew the community, and c) to transform culture.

Talking Points: In your own work experience, what specific connections do you see between worldview beliefs (or assumptions) and the behavior of people you work with?

Chapter Three

The Most Convincing Lie

The title of this chapter poses an intriguing question. What *does* make the most convincing lie?

Governments go to great lengths to design, create, and safeguard money from forgery. If you look at a 20-dollar bill, you'll immediately notice countless details that make it extremely difficult to duplicate.

If someone wanted to counterfeit a 20-dollar bill, the challenge would be to print one that most closely resembles the original. The intent is to deceive, and deception is best accomplished by creating what looks most like the real thing. The most convincing lie is *one that comes as close as possible to the truth.*

What happens if you're unknowingly in possession of a fake bill? At worst you might go to prison for fifteen years, and at best your money will be rejected because it's not the real thing. It may look enough like the truth to convince some people it's valid, but when you take it to the bank, it has zero value, and can land you in a heap of trouble.

In Chapter 2, we said a worldview is: *"a comprehensive framework of beliefs that helps us to interpret what we see and experience, and also gives us direction in the choices that we make as we live out our days."*

The "comprehensive framework" of a worldview consists of five pillars. We saw these five pillars in our working definition of "worldview," namely: *"A worldview is a 'big picture' of reality shaped by beliefs or assumptions about God, Creation, Humanity, Moral Order and Purpose."*

The challenge all followers of Christ face in the workplace is to view our work-life in the context of a bigger picture of reality that's distinctly and radically biblical.

In *GPAW: Bridging the Sacred-Secular Divide* and in the follow-up study, *GPAW: The Difference One Life Can Make,* we will examine twelve pieces of the biblical bigger picture of reality. Of course there are many more than twelve pieces to the biblical big picture, but I believe the twelve that we will look at are the most useful "big picture pieces" in enabling us to see all the smaller pieces of our work-lives in ways that will help us to more fully experience God's pleasure at work, and thus our own pleasure at work, too.

When these twelve Big Picture Pieces are presented in sequential order, they present a narrative, or story, if you will, in four parts: *Creation, Fall, Redemption* and *Restoration.*

All four parts of the narrative are important. But following the cue of someone who wisely suggested, "begin with the end in mind," we'll start by taking a look at the last part of the biblical narrative first, namely: *Restoration.* We'll do this by looking at four Big Picture Pieces relating to this part of the story.

To get started, we'll examine one of the most troublesome counterfeits in Western history. I'm referring to the problem of Western *dualism.*

Dualism is such a deeply ingrained part of Western culture that most Westerners grow up taking it for granted, never questioning it, even though we may never have heard the term articulated. For most of us, it's the only way of seeing reality we have ever known.

Let me unpack the term and explain why dualism is such a problem for followers of Christ who want to fully experience God's pleasure at work.

Dualism is not easy to define. Generally, it is a way of thinking that divides reality into two distinct compartments, with a wide gap between. Dualism divorces science from religion. It divorces our public lives from our private lives. It divorces the corporate world from the personal world. It divorces the material world from the spiritual world. It divorces the body from the soul. It divorces "facts" from "values." And, perhaps the biggest problem for followers of Christ, it divorces the "secular" from the "sacred."

Dualism and biblical worldview do not mix. Or, at least, they *shouldn't* mix. Yet, many people *have* unknowingly mixed dualism with the biblical worldview. And it has had a debilitating effect upon the fuller integration of Christian faith in the workplace by Christ's followers who don't realize how much they have been influenced by it. That's because dualism comes very, very close to the truth. And because it does, it is a very convincing lie.

We need to become "unconvinced." And to get to this point, we'll need to examine the origins of Western dualism, taking a brief look at history, and then linking it with the realities of today's workplace.

Talking Point: Can you give some examples of how dualism expresses itself in the work-world? (Refer to the description of dualism on the previous page, sixth full paragraph.)

SOME IDEAS CAST LONG SHADOWS

Dennis Peacocke, author of *Doing Business God's Way*, has said, "Ideas cast longer shadows than men." This is particularly true of Plato. All Westerners are living in Plato's shadow, even in the 21st Century, though most of us don't give it a second thought. A short DVD clip, called "Plato 101," will provide a brief introduction.

DVD Clip #7
Plato 101
Approx. 3 minutes

Plato's view of reality looks like one of London's double-decker buses. In the lower level is the world of physical matter that comes and goes with the passing of time. This lower, physical realm is constantly changing. Everything that is part of the physical world eventually falls apart. Even the great stone buildings of the ancient Greeks are in ruins today. Nothing is permanent. Nothing lasts. Nothing is eternal. Plants, animals and the bodies of human beings are included in this constant cycle of birth and death.

Prior to Plato, one of the most influential Greek philosophers was Heraclitus, who seemed to be saying the world of matter is in continual flux, and the only constant is change. Plato said Heraclitus' view of the world went like this: "All things go and nothing stays."

But Plato wasn't satisfied with this state of things. He pointed his pupils to another world. A world that was not affected by change. It was the world of the "metaphysical," or "beyond physical." Plato pointed his pupils to a non-physical realm of perfect "ideals" which were not subject to the continual birth and death cycle of the physical, material world.

In the metaphysical realm, Plato's "ideals" are eternal. That is, the "ideals" always were and ever will be. They are universal. They are the same everywhere. Plato referred to the ideal realm of reality as the realm of "form,"in contrast to the realm of "matter."

To better understand the difference between "form" and "matter," let's do a simple exercise.

Draw the best circle you can on a piece of paper. You may draw it free-hand, or you may trace around something circular, such as a coin or the bottom of a cup. Take a moment to do this.

Regardless of how you arrived at it, you just created a new piece of the material world. You created a "particular" circle that is now a part of the world of "matter."

But the particular circle you drew is imperfect (no matter how good an artist you may be). Furthermore, your particular circle is temporal. It won't last forever. It will someday turn to dust.

Yet in order for you to create that *particular* circle, you drew upon a *universal* concept of "circleness." This concept of "circleness" is eternal and unchanging. That is, it the same everywhere, and is unaffected by time or decay. It is an ideal. It is an everlasting "form."

According to Platonism, the universal "form" of "circleness" has more significance than any particular, temporal circle that exists in the world of physical matter.

Plato's "forms" were not just metaphysical concepts of circles, squares, and triangles. He sought to discover ideal "forms" of truth, justice, civil government, goodness and beauty.

Over time, the net effect of Platonism was the notion that the temporal world of matter is *inferior* to the eternal world of forms. The physical pieces of matter consisted only of temporary and imperfect "shadows" of the perfect, ideal "forms" which lie above and beyond the physical, material world.

The important thing to remember here, and the thing that has affected the way many of us view the world of work, is that Plato's division of the physical realm and the metaphysical realm had the net effect of *devaluing* physical matter, and *elevating* ideals.

There is much more to Plato's philosophy than I can share here. In the limited space that I have to deal with these things, I confess I'm indulging in a bit of simplification and exaggeration to make a point. But I'm not oversimplifying and exaggerating all that much!

Plato's ideas were put into his writings, and his philosophy gained a large following in the ancient world. What's more, Platonism had a lasting effect on Western thought in general, right up to the present hour.

TRUE OR FALSE?

Let's take a moment to look at some statements rooted in platonic thought. As you read the statements below, place a letter "T" in front of each statement you think is in *harmony* with Scripture, and a letter "F" in front of any statements you think are in *conflict* with what the Bible teaches:

1. Some things are temporal and pass away, while other things are eternal and never decay.
2. It is vain to live your life for the pursuit of material things.
3. Temporal things do not have real significance.
4. Only eternal things have true value.
5. The eternal world is a place to which we escape.
6. The body is the prison house of the soul.

I don't know what you came up with, but I submit that only statements 1 and 2 are fully biblical. Some of the rest may be partially biblical, depending on how you interpret the question. But they are more false than true.

Talking Point: Do you agree that *only* statements 1 and 2 are fully biblical? Support your position whether you do or do not agree.

Maybe you agree that only statements 1 and 2 are biblical, and maybe you don't. But whether you do or you don't, I'm going to assume that some people reading this book will question my conclusion—or at least you will want to know *why* I say only statements 1 and 2 are truly biblical.

Let me begin my defense by presenting the first Big Picture Piece of that part of the biblical narrative we call Restoration: *We live in a fallen world, which is not the way it was originally made to be, but we do not live in a forsaken world.*

ALL GOD'S STUFF IS GOOD

In the beginning, God created the heavens and the earth. But that's not all there was to it. He not only created the material world at a given point in the past, but He actively upholds and sustains that material world through time, including the present moment.

In Colossians 1:16-17, Paul wrote: "For it was in Him *[that is, in Christ]* that all things were created, in heaven and on earth, things seen and things unseen, whether thrones, dominions, rulers or authorities; all things were created *and exist* through Him and in and for Him. And He Himself existed before all things, and in Him all things consist *[cohere, are held together].*" I added the emphasis from the Amplified Bible.

Notice how many times the word "things" appears in these two verses. Six times. Also, notice that in Christ [the Creator], all things "cohere," or are "held together." This includes the chair you are sitting on, and it includes your own body!

Temporal or not, all matter is being held together by God. All of it! And it only continues to exist through time and space because He is continually sustaining it by His command.

Any interaction, therefore, with temporal matter, in the form of *work*, is interaction with that which God is holding together. And what's more, the Bible says it is *good* stuff, as He declared in Genesis 1.

Talking Point: All work, to one degree or another, deals with "things." What specific things that God created do you primarily deal with in your line of work?

ALL GOD'S STUFF IS HIS

In Paul's famous marketplace message to Athen's pagan philosophers, as he stood on a very large outcrop called "Mars Hill," he pronounced: *"God, who made the world and everything in it…gives to all life, breath, and all things…In Him we live and move and have our being…"* (Acts 17:24-28)

What's noteworthy here is that Paul is not addressing a group of Christians. He is speaking to non-believing Greek philosophers.

This prompts an important question: Is Paul saying that *non-*

believers "live and move and have their being in Christ?"

Yes he is. In a physical, material sense, *everyone* lives and moves and has their being in Christ. He is the Great Sustainer.

As we've already seen in Col. 1:17, "...in Him all things are held together." And in Hebrews 1:3, the writer says that Christ is "upholding all things by the word of His power." *All things* is pretty inclusive.

What I am touching on here is what theologians call "Common Grace." God is sustaining the breath of the atheist as well as the Christian. He sends life-giving rain on the just and the unjust.

But there's more. Not only is God continually sustaining the material world, He *owns* it! As the psalmist reminds us in Psalm 24:1, "The earth *is the Lord's* and *all* its fullness, the world *and those who dwell therein.*" [Emphasis mine.]

To put it plainly, all non-believers are "the Lord's possession," whether they have a personal relationship with Him or not. This is what makes the separation of human beings from fellowship with God such a tragic thing. It is *God's possession* that is separated from Him!

Talking Point: Do you often think of the people you work with as "God's own possession?" Do these people seem different to you when you think about them in this way?

ALL GOD'S STUFF IS SIGNIFICANT

This brings us to the next Big Picture Piece with respect to Restoration: *The earth and everything in it remains God's own possession, and therefore it has great significance.*

By virtue of God's creation, *all* forms of matter, including people, are God's own stuff. So, as we stroll down the street, drive our cars, or walk through our places of business, we can think of each and every individual we pass as *"God's own possession."* It makes a difference in how we interact with them. It gives them extraordinary significance.

Think about it. Every non-believer you work with, whether co-worker, customer or client, is God's own possession: "The earth is the Lord's, and every thing in it...the world and *all who live in it.*"

It's worth being redundant on this point, so I will be: your co-workers who have not trusted in Christ's substitutionary death on their behalf, and who are separated from union with Christ, are God's own possession by virtue of creation. God is sustaining their breath moment by moment, regardless of their attitude, and regardless of their behavior. They may deny God's very existence, or curse Him daily. But they are sustained by God and are His own possessions.

This truth has massive implications for how we relate to the people we work for, and work with, every single day.

Bear in mind that it's not only *people* who are God's own possession, it's every other part of the world of matter as well.

In short, the biblical worldview has a very high regard for the physical (yes, even temporal) world of matter in which we all live and work. The implications of this for farmers, iron workers, and car mechanics are huge. Not to mention the implications for CEOs and homemakers.

This temporal world is God's world. Physical matter is good. All God's stuff is significant. If it were not, why would He keep holding it together? It has a worthy purpose. It is "meant to be." God hasn't devalued it. Yes, He will make a new earth at some point in the future, but we dare not conclude from this that God has abandoned the current material world, or that it is of no real value to Him. If we think this, we'll miss God's pleasure in working with temporal things.

Talking Point: What is the significance of the physical things that you buy, sell, manage or create in your line of work? (Perhaps a better way to pose the question is, "What significance does *God* see in the material things you work with?")

WHAT NOW?

If you discovered you were carrying some counterfeit money, I assume you'd do whatever you could to hand it over to the authorities as quickly as possible.

In the same way, if you're carrying a counterfeit worldview, one that devalues the temporal, material world, I encourage you to reconsider your assumptions, and to do whatever you can to rid yourself of this false "currency."

In Chapter 4, we'll go deeper into this process, as we look at how Western dualism led to a split view of reality that divides life into "sacred" and "secular" compartments. We'll discuss how we can view work in a way that doesn't divide people's occupations into "sacred" and "secular" endeavors, and we'll ask the all-important question, *"does the secular world even exist?"*

Chapter Four

Bridging the Sacred-Secular Divide

When we hear the word "worship," we often think about what goes on at church on Sunday mornings. So it might sound a bit strange if I were to suggest to you that a man sanding a hardwood floor could be engaged in authentic worship, too.

I don't mean he might be humming a hymn while he is working. I mean he could be engaged in authentic worship *in the action of sanding a hardwood floor.*

I'll go even further. A man sanding a hardwood floor *could* be engaged in more authentic worship than a man singing a hymn at church on Sunday morning. For if while I'm singing a hymn my mind is thinking about the fishing trip I'm taking next Friday, or the football game I'll be watching that afternoon, but while I'm sanding a hardwood floor on Monday morning I do this work "heartily as unto the Lord," I am *not* worshipping in the former scenario, but I *am* worshipping in the latter.

Authentic worship depends on what's going on inside my head and my heart. To understand how sanding a floor can be authentic "worship" requires a clear definition of *worship.*

If we can rid our minds of Western dualism long enough to give some serious reflection to the meaning of "worship," we can realize how physical work may truly be a spiritual activity. The body and the soul should not be divorced in our minds. It is entirely possible to engage with the temporal, material world in such a way that our engagement incorporates direct service to God. And it is possible (I should say *desirable*) for humans to be engaged in spiritual worship *by means of* the physical body and the material creation.

In Romans 12:1 Paul writes: *"I appeal to you therefore, brothers, by the mercies of God, to present your bodies as a living sacrifice, holy and acceptable to God, which is your spiritual worship."*

Here there is no divorcing of the spirit from the body. Rather, we see a unified whole. We see our spiritual worship in the context of our presentation of the body.

This isn't difficult to imagine when we think of singers using their vocal cords to sing to the Lord, or clapping our hands to the beat of a lively chorus at church. We can also see it in King David dancing before the Lord with all his might.

But could "presenting one's body as a living sacrifice, acceptable to God" also include the physical action of sanding a hardwood floor? Could sanding a hardwood floor be a spiritual exercise as well as a physical exercise?

Talking Point: Could it be?

Col. 3:23 tells us: *"Whatever you do, do your work heartily, as for the Lord rather than for men…"* Clearly the Scripture makes room for physical labor (and mental labor, for that matter) to be God-centered, and God-directed. A man sanding a hardwood floor "for the Lord" *could* be participating in worship every bit as much as a man or woman singing in church. Maybe more so.

The fact of the matter is work provides countless opportunities for us to offer our bodies as living sacrifices, "holy and acceptable to God," which is nothing less than a spiritual act of authentic worship. Try doing this the next time you mow your lawn, or wash the dishes.

The man who sands a hardwood floor "for the Lord" is the man who is sanding a floor as though Jesus was to be the resident of the house. Let me say it again: he is sanding the floor as though Jesus were going to walk on it.

Now that's worship! This changes the man's focus from simply "doing a job" and "getting a paycheck," to "building a cathedral." This is the man who is truly bringing meaning to his work.

Of course, this way of thinking doesn't just apply to the person who does the physical labor of sanding the floor. It applies just as much to the people behind the scenes, such as the bankers, architects, makers of tools, sellers of building materials, and so on. Every participant at every level of the process *can* be engaged in authentic spiritual worship when the work he or she does is done "as for the Lord."

If you cannot really do your work "as for the Lord," you might consider finding another line of work in which you can. But before you quit your day job, bear in mind that there are very few kinds of work that cannot be done "as for the Lord." Nearly any work, with the exception of illegal work, can be done "as for the Lord."

Talking Point: Are you convinced that *your* work can be authentic worship when it is done "as for the Lord?" Exactly *how* can your particular work be done "for the Lord?"

IDEAS HAVE CONSEQUENCES

Here's an idea that could have extraordinary consequences for the course of history, if we take it to heart: the physical world has significance for God — *and thus for us!*

Work is simply governance or stewardship over some aspect of God's very significant, temporal, material world. Work brings order to as yet unordered things; it brings shape to as yet shapeless things. Most importantly, work is the means by which we fulfill *the first commission God gave to human beings.*

Most readers are probably familiar with the *Great* Commission, in Matthew 28, where Jesus sends his disciples into all the world to make more disciples. But what is The *First* Commission?

The First Commission is found in Genesis Chapter 1:26-28, where God said: *"Let us make man in our image, in our likeness, and let them rule...over all the earth."*

In Chapter 2 of Genesis, verse 15, we see God following through with His plan: *"Then the Lord God took the man and put him in the garden of Eden, to tend and keep it."*

There is great significance in the fact that God created us in His likeness and image, and then commissioned us to rule over His creation. The only reason we are able to govern and rule over the material world is because we have been equipped to do so *as image-bearers of God.*

It is important to note that the "tending and keeping" Adam did in Eden occurred *prior* to the entrance of sin in the world. Work is not a result of sin. Work is not a curse! Work was part of God's original intention for humanity long before sin entered the picture. Our work is just harder because of sin. But God intended people to do the "tending and keeping" right from the start.

The First Commission is sometimes called the "Cultural Mandate." Why? Because it is a mandate to create culture out of the material world that God spoke into existence and commissioned us to manage.

Because of the entrance of sin into the world, and because this current earth God has created is going to be burned up someday, some may ask, "Should we bother to polish brass on a sinking ship?"

This is a valid question. Why *should* followers of Christ be concerned about governing over a fallen world of physical matter? Why *should* we be concerned with making buildings, growing snow peas, and manufacturing computers?

Why?

We should concern ourselves with governing over this physical, material world *because God created and commissioned us to do exactly that!*

The answer to the question "Why did God make us?" is not terribly difficult. The answer is right there in the first chapter of Genesis. *He made us to rule over this planet.*

Of course, this doesn't answer the next big question, "*Why* did He create us to rule over this planet?" This is more of a mystery. But knowing that we were created for the express purpose of governing over the earth is enough knowledge for us to deal with for now. It will keep us busy for quite some time.

The Big Picture Piece we're talking about here is this: "*The First Commission given by God to humans is to govern over all the earth.*"

This Big Picture Piece encapsulates one of the most profoundly far-reaching ideas of Scripture. *We were created in the likeness and image of God so that we could rule over this physical, material world. And when we work, we are putting our likeness of God to work in fulfilling our primary job description.*

Talking Point: Specifically, *how* does *your* particular work serve to fulfill the First Commission?

A HIGH VIEW OF THE PHYSICAL WORLD

A high view of the physical world and our role in it led the ancient Hebrews to take a much different view of physical labor than did the ancient Greeks. The next DVD clip will help explain what I'm talking about.

DVD Clip #8
A Positive View of Matter
Approx. 3.5 minutes

The fact that in Jesus' day a rabbi was expected to know not only the books of the Law, but to be also proficient at a physical trade is significant. As I wrote extensively in *Assumptions That Affect Our Lives*, Westerners have been more influenced by the ancient Greeks than we realize. In general, we, like the ancient Greeks, tend to elevate the "thinking professions," such as lawyers, doctors and college professors, and not give as much respect to those who do manual labor.

As it is often translated into the church world, we tend to elevate the work of those who are in "the ministry," and not give a lot of attention to those whose ministry is providing excellent floors for people's homes, or sinks in which people may brush their teeth.

At Jesus' baptism, when the Father declared, *"This is My beloved Son in whom I am well pleased,"* bear in mind that at this point in His life, Jesus had not preached a single sermon to the masses, nor healed a single person, nor done a single miracle.

I dare say God the Father was as well-pleased with Jesus throughout the many years Jesus spent as a carpenter as He was throughout the three years Jesus spent as an itinerant teacher.

Talking Point: Do you agree with this last statement? If you do or do not, support your position biblically.

Jesus spent about *six times* as much time doing carpentry work than He did preaching. In either case, Jesus did His work "unto God." He only did what the Father showed Him to do, and this included at least sixteen years of work as a carpenter.

CHANGING OUR MINDS

In order for Christ's followers today to actually believe that God can be as pleased with people doing carpentry as He is with people preaching, or feeding the hungry, we must rid ourselves of any semblance of Western dualism.

The next DVD clip will get us started.

DVD Clip #9
Detachment From Matter
Approx. 2 minutes

The mixture of Platonism with Christianity eventually led to a religious dualism in which all of life was divided into higher and lower spheres. Today we call things in the upper sphere "sacred," and in the lower sphere, "secular."

In the "sacred" compartment of our minds, we put things pertaining to the spiritual, eternal realm of "God's affairs," or "things related to religion." In the "secular" compartment of our minds, we put things pertaining to the physical and temporal realm of "man's affairs," or, "things not related to religion."

Now, some might say, "Isn't this the way it is? Doesn't the sacred part of life have to do with things like prayer, Bible study, singing hymns, evangelism, and the church? Doesn't the secular part of life have to do with Monday-through-Friday work at

Microsoft, or Starbucks, or a government office?"

I once looked up the word "secular" in a dictionary and found it defined as *"not related to religion."* And in the same dictionary, "religion" was defined as *"a system of beliefs centering on a supernatural being."*

Now, let's think this through a bit. If *all* physical matter is held together (right now) "by the word of His power," can there be *any* sphere of reality that exists in a vacuum, separated from God's awareness and presiding power? Is there any part of life that functions "on its own?" Is there any part of life *not* related in some way to the centrality and supremacy of Christ? Can there be any part of life that doesn't pertain to "God's affairs?"

Talking Point: *Can* there be? Support your position.

I don't think so.

Whether people acknowledge it or not, or whether they realize it or not, Christ *is* the center of everything. And He doesn't need our permission to be so. Jesus *is* Lord of all, whether people recognize Him as such or not. And if this is true, then I submit to you there can be no place called the "secular" world.

If this sounds a bit odd to your ears, the next DVD clip may help clarify things.

DVD Clip #10
Where is the Secular World?
Approx. 3.5 minutes

Here's what Dallas Willard has to say about the supposed sacred-secular divide:

"There is truly no division between sacred and secular except what we have created. And that is why the division of the legitimate roles and functions of human life into the sacred and secular does incalculable damage to our individual lives and to the cause of Christ. Holy

people must...take up holy orders in farming, industry, law, education, banking, and journalism with the same zeal previously given to evangelism or to pastor and missionary work."

If we want to rid ourselves of dualism, I suggest we drop the word "secular" from our vocabulary. Why? Because every time we use the word, we legitimize the concept.

If you feel you must use the word "secular," try substituting the word *"secularized."* For example, while we can't say we live in a "secular" world, we can say we live in a *"secularized"* world. While we can't say we have a "secular" job, we can say we have a *"secularized"* job, if we have a job in which the workers habitually leave God out of the picture. And if that's the case, perhaps we can "de-secularize" our occupations by bringing Him into the picture—at least within our own minds and spheres of responsibility. After all, He is always there anyway. We can ignore Him, *but we can't remove Him.* He's holding it all together!

We'll take a closer look at how to rid ourselves of dualism in Chapter 5. But first, take time to reflect on what you have read.

Talking Point: Are you personally convinced that the "secular" world does not really exist? Why or why not?

Are you personally convinced that you do not have a "secular" job? Why or why not?

Chapter Five

Viewing Work Through a Different Lens

In this chapter, we'll look at a faulty view of work that the West has come to accept as "normal," and introduce an alternative view which, if embraced, will help all of us to recover from the debilitating effects of dualism.

In Chapter 2, you viewed a short segment of a report that ABC News did on John Beckett, Chairman of The Beckett Companies, that demonstrated how his biblical worldview shaped the culture of his company.

Now I'd like you to view the full report, because it illustrates what can happen when a business leader stops compartmentalizing things into sacred and secular categories, and views life as a unified whole under the lordship of Christ, the Creator-Sustainer of all things.

This 1995 television report was seen by an estimated 12 million people, and it prompted more calls to ABC News than any previous feature news story they had produced.

DVD Clip #11
ABC News: "Faith in the Workplace"
Approx. 5 minutes

Talking Point: What particularly impressed you about the ABC News segment you have just viewed?

In the late 1980's, a friend of John Beckett recommended that he read my book, *Assumptions That Affect Our Lives* (then titled, *Different Windows*). In this book there is a section on the roots of dualism, and the effects this way of thinking has had on Christians for hundreds of years. In that same section of the *Assumptions* book, an alternative way of viewing things is presented, in line with a biblical paradigm, or a biblical way of seeing.

This material on dualism, and how to replace it with the biblical alternative, had a transformational effect on John Beckett's thinking. I'll elaborate on the biblical alternative in a few moments. But before I do, I'd like you to view a short segment of a video interview I did with John Beckett in his Elyria office, in 2002, seven years after the ABC News piece was broadcast. Here he elaborates on what struck him most about the biblical alternative to dualism, and why it made a difference in his approach to work in general, and to his own work in particular.

DVD Clip #12
John Beckett on The Biblical Alternative to Dualism
Approx. 3 minutes

A few years after the ABC News story came out, John Beckett wrote a book called, *Loving Monday*. In this book he shared his personal epiphany regarding work as a noble calling, and the realization that his own work as a manufacturer of oil burners was significant in the sight of God. Here's the way he put it:

"When I saw this distinction — this contrast in worldviews — I wanted to do cartwheels. If I hadn't grown up as a proper Episcopalian, I probably would have! I realized how much my thinking had been negatively affected by Greek dualism.

In stark contrast to my prior thinking, the Bible enabled me to view my work as having great worth to God, provided I would bring it into harmony with Him in every way possible. As a believer and a business person, I was no longer a second-class citizen. Nor did I need to leave my Christian convictions and biblical values outside the office entrance when I headed into work on Monday mornings.

A biblical worldview has awesome implications…As we allow it, the Bible speaks to us concerning government, economics, education, science, art, communications and yes, business. Really, it speaks to all of life."

The simple diagram below captures the essence of the biblical alternative to the "sacred-secular split." It is based upon the work of Albert Wolters, in his excellent book, *Creation Regained*, which I recommend you read in concert with *Loving Monday*:

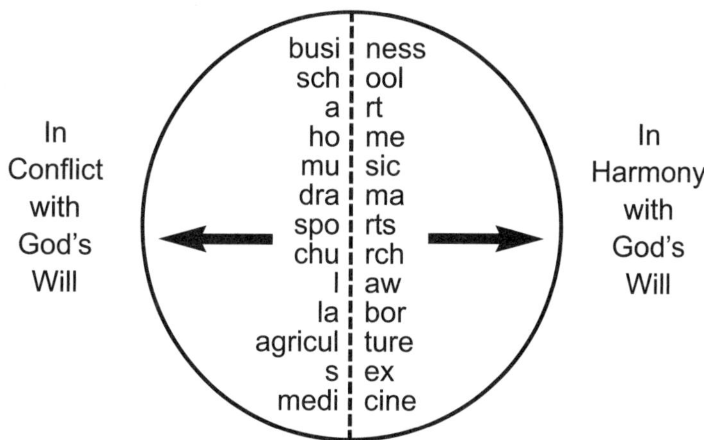

One can list every major sphere of life down the middle of the circle, from business, to politics, to medicine, to the media. You name it. Any activity listed can either be done in a manner that is in *harmony* with God or in *conflict* with God.

Any business on planet Earth can fulfill God's purposes, or oppose God's purposes. Political activity can be done in harmony with the kingdom of light, or in line with the domain of darkness. The same can be said for art, music, literature, sports, and even church activity. Any form of work done by human beings can be pulled to one side or the other, in harmony or in conflict with God's will.

The issue, then, has nothing to do with whether or not a particular kind of work is "sacred" or "secular," but whether it is done in a way that is honoring to God or dishonoring to God. Here there is no horizontal "split" into "upper" and "lower" spheres (as we have in the Greek model) but a vertical distinction between that which is in *harmony* with God or in *conflict* with God.

Talking Point: Does this way of seeing things cause you to see your particular work differently than you did before?

Although creation is *one* realm, belonging entirely to God, made of matter sustained through time by that same Creator, we also live in a *fallen* world, where evil does exist. Living in a world that is sustained by God and where evil is also found may sound like a contradiction. We'll discuss this mystery in more detail in *GPAW: The Difference One Life Can Make*, when we talk about the Fall and the Kingdom of God.

But for now, just hang on to the idea that as followers of Christ we can bring our work into alignment with God's purposes through a very wide variety of occupations. *A variety as wide as creation itself!* And when we bring our work into alignment with God's will, we bring Christ's light to darkened places.

When we create oil burners for the Lord, when we repair cars for the Lord, when we cook food, drive trucks, sell shoes, and make computer software for the Lord, we can have a dramatic effect on our workplaces, and our culture at large. While few of us are in CEO positions, we all have a sphere of influence within which we can align our faith with our work.

All of this leads to another Big Picture Piece: *God purposes to do His will on earth as it is in heaven, and by His grace He will work through redeemed people to bring His light to every sphere of life.*

Our role as humans is to engage in The First Commission. This can be done in whatever sphere of creation we put our hands and minds to work, realizing there is no sphere of creation exempt from the call of The First Commission. God has given us a job description as broad as creation is wide.

Of course we're dealing with temporal stuff! So what? It's *His* temporal stuff! We won't achieve perfection in this life, but by God's grace, we can align our work with God's design for fish, for trees, for gold, for soybeans and for oil burners.

In John Beckett's corporate world, it means aligning the purposes of God with employee benefits, co-worker relationships, marketing, decision-making policies, product quality, pricing, contracts, global trade, hiring and firing, accounting, management issues, environmental impact, strategic planning, profit distribution and community service. And when Beckett does these things in harmony with God's will and ways it benefits everyone. It also brings honor and glory to the Lord—not to mention a great deal of joy to Beckett himself. He is loving Monday for many good reasons.

We dare not call John Beckett's work "secular." You see, it's *God's work* to help keep people warm in the winter, and it's *God's work* to provide jobs for hundreds of people in northern Ohio. These are jobs that provide the means for parents to raise their families, and jobs that generate taxes to build roads and assure legitimate civil services, not to mention generating offerings that allow local churches to keep their doors open.

Talking Point: Do you agree that it is "God's work" to help keep people warm in the winter? Support your position.

Let's wrap up this chapter with another short segment from my interview with John Beckett.*

DVD Clip #13
John Beckett on Authenticity
Approx. 2 minutes

Talking Point: What will be your primary "take-away" from this chapter?

To view a more in-depth interview of John Beckett by Peggy Wheymeyer, visit www.secretsofsuccess.com/videos. It is excellent. Other inspiring examples of "faith-at-work" are on this site. In addition, please visit www.iquestions.com/browse/faculty/johnbeckett to view John Beckett answering important business-and-faith-related questions. You'll be glad you did.

Chapter Six

Have You Ever Seen a "Secular" Color?

We often hear the term "secular music" applied to the kind of music we don't hear in church, or the term "secular art" applied to paintings hanging on the office wall. But what exactly makes art or music "secular?" Is it the lyrics? The subject matter? The publisher? The beat?

Hopefully, based on what we've discussed in Chapter 4, you will be hard-pressed to come up with a valid rationale for tagging *any* art or music as "secular." We should instead ask, "is it *good* music?" And by "good," I mean, is it *honoring to God, pleasing to the Lord,* and *a blessing to humanity.* That's the way I see it, anyway.

Now why would I include a chapter on the arts in a book that deals with work? Contrary to what some may think, it *is* possible to have a "real" job as an artist or a musician. Lots of people make their living working in some form of the arts. Furthermore, producing good art is very hard work.

But beyond these things, all of us are touched on a daily basis by art, whether it is in the form of music, graphic design, or fine arts. A work-world without the arts would be a very dreary place indeed.

In this chapter, we'll focus on how we can bridge the "sacred-secular divide" with respect to the arts. As we discussed in Chapter 4, one of the great challenges we have as followers of Christ in a Greek-ish culture is to remove the sacred-secular split from our thinking.

The best way to get rid of this split view is to replace it with a different view. Specifically, in the case of the arts, we need to replace the sacred-secular, "higher-lower" view, with the idea presented in Chapter 5, which looks like the chart below when applied to the arts:

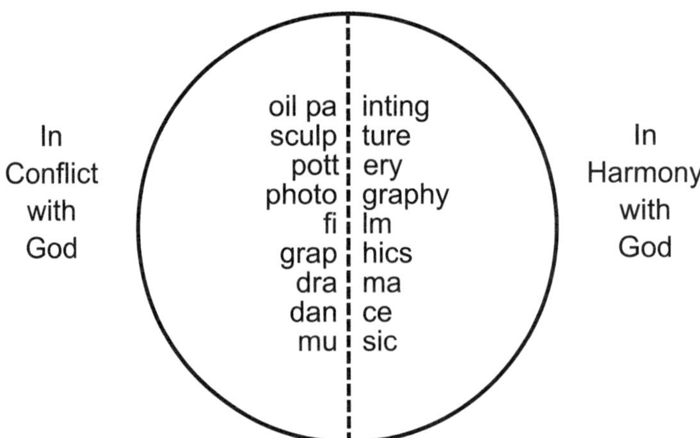

Any sphere of human activity in the arts can be done in a manner that is in harmony with God or out of harmony with Him. But the raw material is God's stuff. He is holding together all the oil paint of the world by the word of His power. No color is secular. It's God's own possession. He is sustaining every sound wave that comes from every musical instrument.

While the raw materials are one thing, what human beings *do* with these raw materials is another thing. Sometimes what people do with the raw materials is honoring to the Lord, and sometimes it is not. More often than not, it is a mixture.

Talking Point: Can you give some examples of art, music, film, etc., that are honoring to the Lord, but not generally classified as "Christian?" What examples can you give of art, music or film that is a *mixture* of being honoring to the Lord and being dishonoring to Him?

PLEASANT TO THE SIGHT

God has an eye for beauty. He cares about it. And because we are created in His likeness and image, people like good art. We are affected by it, and God knows it.

It is significant to note that when God created trees, He didn't create them just to produce fruit for humans to eat. He had more in mind. Genesis 2:8-9a says: *"The Lord God planted a garden eastward in Eden, and there He put the man whom He had formed. And out of the ground the Lord God made every tree grow that is pleasant to the sight and good for food."* [New King James Version]

Imagine that. God didn't make trees just for utilitarian purposes, that is, just to give us food. He also made trees *to give us pleasure* through our sense of sight. He didn't have to do this! But I'm glad He did.

We don't *have* to hang a beautiful painting in the hallway, or put a fountain in the entry, but it sure can be pleasant to the senses for all who enter. And this is another way we (and others) can experience God's pleasure at work: we can experience *His* pleasure in giving *us* pleasure!

In Exodus 28:2, we read that God instructed Moses to make garments for Aaron, his brother the priest, *"for glory and for beauty."* The robes were not just functional. They were pleasing to the sight.

In verses 31-34 of that chapter, we're given more details: *"You shall make the robe of the ephod all of blue...it shall have a woven binding all around its opening...And upon its hem you shall make pomegranates of blue, purple, and scarlet, all around its hem, and bells of gold between them all around: a golden bell and a pomegranate, a golden bell and a pomegranate, upon the hem of the robe all around."* [New King James Version]

Blue pomegranates? Have you ever seen blue pomegranates? I haven't. But the Lord instructed people to sew blue pomegranates next to purple and scarlet ones for the sake of beauty.

WISE ART

In the chapter of Exodus where God prescribes blue pomegranates for Aaron's robe, He also says to Moses: *"So you shall speak to all who are gifted artisans, whom I have filled with the spirit of wisdom, that they may make Aaron's garments..."*

What is noteworthy here, is the fact that God filled artisans with *"the spirit of wisdom"* for the task of making clothing. That's a different sort of wisdom than usually comes to mind when we hear the word "wisdom." We usually think of *words* of wisdom, or wise *counsel*. But here we see another sort of wisdom: *wise clothing design.*

This kind of wisdom isn't limited just to clothing design. In Exodus 31:2-4, God says: *"See, I have called by name Bezalel the son of Uri, the son of Hur, of the tribe of Judah. And I have filled him with the Spirit of God, in wisdom, in understanding, in knowledge, and in all manner of workmanship, to design artistic works, to work in gold, in silver, in bronze, in cutting jewels for setting, in carving wood, and to work in all manner of workmanship."* [New King James Version]

All manner of workmanship? That's what it says. Could this apply to a man sanding hardwood floors? I think so.

What's very interesting about Exodus 31:2-4 is the fact that this is the first recorded instance in the Bible of a man being *filled with the Spirit.* And for what purpose? To preach? To heal? To prophesy? No. To design artwork!

Talking Point: Have you ever heard someone being prayed for to be filled with the Spirit so they could produce good art? If not, why do you think this is the case? If so, when?

If you are an artisan, when was the last time you *asked* to be filled with the Spirit so that you could work skillfully with paint, film, jewels, or wood? Imagine being blessed with the same kind of understanding, wisdom, knowledge and craftsmanship that God gave Bezalel!

Wouldn't it be something if artists, musicians and filmmakers in the Body of Christ were to be commissioned by their local churches to produce great artwork? I'm not talking about paying them to do some artwork for the church, although that would be appropriate. Rather, I'm talking about setting them apart through the laying on of the leadership's hands, to be filled with the Spirit for the purposes of God to be accomplished through their artistic work in the world, and doing this with as much seriousness as we would for the next missionary couple flying off to Africa. For that matter, why not include the floor sanders, too?

Of course, I'm not suggesting we single out the artisans any more than we single out the missionaries. Any working person in good standing with the church who truly desires to be set apart for the purposes of God to be fulfilled through his or her daily work could conceivably be commissioned for service, couldn't they?

Talking Point: Do you think that commissioning followers of Christ publicly in the way that has been described here (no matter what work they do), is a good idea or not a good idea? If you think it is a good idea, under what guidelines? If not, why not?

For the artist who wants to serve Christ by producing works of art that glorify the Lord, it does not mean that he or she is limited to painting white doves on church steeples. The whole realm of creation is God's canvas, and so is the canvas of the Christ-following artist.

By the way, the artist who is an atheist is also an image-bearer of God, and thus he or she is able to produce good art. Only an image-bearer of God can lift brush to canvas and reproduce his or her own face. Good art inherently glorifies God, because only image-bearers of God, made in His likeness, can create good art. And there is a lot of music out there that is pleasing to God, even though the composers who wrote it may not personally know the Lord.

THE DEVIL'S BLACK BOX?

My great grandmother was a very committed believer in Christ who referred to the radio as "The Devil's Black Box." She was alive when it was invented, and apparently felt the radio would be used to further the domain of darkness. Well, at times the radio has been used this way. But it is God who created and sustains all radio waves, and whether His waves are used in an honorable or dishonorable way will be determined by what human beings put on them.

Television is no different. What is broadcast on God's TV waves can either be in line with the domain of darkness or in line with the kingdom of light. But this doesn't mean followers of Christ should avoid working in the television and film industries. Just the opposite! It means we need Christ-followers in this field who are bringing radio and TV waves into harmony with "good" programming. And again, by "good," I mean, honoring to God, pleasing to the Lord, and a blessing to humanity.

Regrettably, since the days of my great grandmother, many Christians have distanced themselves from careers in radio, television and film, thinking they would be "selling out" spiritually if they went to work in those fields. But for some, it could be just the opposite. To *not* go into such a field might be, as Eric Liddell put it in the film *Chariots of Fire,* "to hold Him in contempt."

We should certainly be encouraging followers of Christ who are able to experience God's pleasure at work through creating music, art and film. We need them in that field as much as anywhere else.

Talking Point: Do you agree with that last statement? Are there any particular words of advice , or caution, you would give to someone wanting to go into the arts or the media as a profession?

Phil Cooke is a producer and director in the television and film industry who is finding God's pleasure at work in Los Angeles. I spoke with Phil on the phone about his work, and I'd like you to listen to his comments that relate to what you are reading in this chapter.

DVD Clip #14
Phil Cooke on The Influence of TV and Film
Approx. 2 minutes

Yes, we do need to come to grips with the fact that television has more significant influence on most young people today than pastors do.

Some producers of TV and film claim that their shows don't influence people's behavior. But Bill Cosby had it right when he said: "The networks say they don't influence anybody. If that's true, why do they have commercials?"

I suspect that if large numbers of followers of Christ had been commissioned by the Church years ago to create wise works of art in the arena of television and film, perhaps the industry wouldn't be quite the field of nightmares it is today.

But it isn't too late. There remains opportunity for followers of Christ to experience God's pleasure at work by creating truly wise art, film, and music.

Talking Point: If you were a television or film director, what specific "wise program or movie" would you like to create?

Chapter Seven

God's Co-Worker

We have considered God's awesome grace in continuously sustaining the realm of matter, upholding it "by the word of His power," and we have considered the fact that He extends His "common grace" to men, women, and children, whether they accept and embrace Him as Lord or not. This "common grace" manifests itself in countless ways, from providing plants to produce oxygen for us to breathe, to positioning the earth a perfect distance from the sun, to giving us the daily food we eat.

Did I say *"giving"* us daily food? Yes. But not directly. You see, God *could* have chosen to deliver the food to our front door Himself, fully cooked, but instead we see a long human chain that links the farmer to the soil, the truck driver to the marketplace, and the grocery clerk to the cash register. All along the way, from one end of the chain to the other, human beings are engaged in The First Commission, whether they realize it or not.

If we continue to follow the chain out the grocery store door, we find men and women who spend 40-60 hours a week at jobs that generate the dollars that are paid at the cash register. And if we go back once again to the other end of the chain, to where the farmer meets the soil, we discover that in the plants, sunshine and rain, things are happening that only God can do. Thus, in the final analysis, it is God who is ultimately to be thanked for giving us our daily bread. And this explains why most followers of Christ take a moment to thank Him before they put fork to mouth.

As humans, we have been designed and commissioned to work. It is a good thing to work. But this process is not only a human one. We are really *co-workers* with God. The milkman delivers the milk that comes from cows and grass that God sustains. Furthermore, it is God who is sustaining the very body and breath of the milkman!

The process that God uses to give you your next breakfast is a delightful dance between Himself and human beings. He sustains the milkman who provides the drink, the butcher who provides the bacon, and the baker who provides the toast. These are all means by which God fulfills His design for food, His love for people, and His intention for humans to work *with* Him to accomplish His purposes in the earth.

In this chapter, we'll look at a great scientist who was able to engage in God's pleasure at work because he fully understood his role as a co-worker with God. He ignored the "sacred-secular split," and, with the help of God, came up with 300 products from the lowly peanut, and 118 products from the humble sweet potato. I'm referring, of course, to Dr. George Washington Carver, who worked with God in his laboratory, which he affectionately called, "God's Little Workshop," unlocking the secrets of legumes for the benefit of humanity.

Take a look at this DVD clip to learn more about the man.

DVD Clip #15
An Introduction to Dr. George Washington Carver
Approx. 4.5 minutes

Talking Point: What was most impressive to you about the DVD clip you just viewed?

A major cable TV channel did a one-hour documentary on the life of George Washington Carver in which they referred to Carver and his accomplishments as a "modern marvel." In the entire program, there was not a single mention of Carver's faith, other than when one of Carver's former students, an elderly gentleman, alluded to Carver's faith in a brief interview.

I once taught the *God's Pleasure At Work* course to a group of businessmen in Bellevue, Washington, where I live. After I shared about the work of Dr. Carver, one man in the group said he had been a student at Iowa State University, where Carver earned a degree in agriculture and became the first African American faculty member at that institution. My friend went on to say that while Carver and his work were prominently displayed at the University, he had no knowledge whatsoever of Carver's faith. Amazingly, this vital aspect of Carver's life was either minimized or totally omitted from the displays.

With a little research, however, one can find several books that reveal this important part of Carver's life. Two such books are, *George Washington Carver: His Life & Faith in His Own Words*, by William J. Federer, published by Amerisearch, Inc., St. Louis, MO, and *Fruits of Creation*, by John S. Ferrell, published by Macalester Park, Shakopee, MN.

In a letter Carver wrote to some friends in Montana, Mr. and Mrs. Milholland, at the age of 26, he said: *"Oh how I wish the people would wake up from their lethargy and come out soul and body for Christ."* He continued: *"Let us pray that the Lord will completely guide us in all things, and that we may gladly be led by Him."* (Federer p. 23)

In a speech given at the age of 59, Carver said: *"God is going to reveal to us things He never revealed before if we put our hands in His."* (Federer p. 53) Carver locked the door to his lab when he was creating things. He claimed, "Only alone can I draw close enough to God to discover His secrets." (Federer, 53)

He wrote a letter to Rev. Lyman Ward, in which he included these telling words: *"Pray for me please that everything said and done will be to His glory. I am not interested in science or anything else that leaves God out of it."* (Federer p. 56)

At age 60, Carver wrote the following to Robert Johnson: *"Living for others is really the Christ life after all. Oh, the satisfaction, happiness and joy one gets out of it...I know that my redeemer lives. Thank God I love humanity; complexion doesn't interest me one single bit."* (Federer p. 57)

At age 63, he wrote: *"Man, who needed a purpose, a mission, to keep him alive, had one. He could be...God's co-worker...My purpose alone must be God's purpose...As I worked on projects which fulfilled a real human need, forces were working through me which amazed me. I would often go to sleep with an apparently insoluble problem. When I woke the answer was there."* In the same letter he declared: *"After I leave this world, I do not believe I am through."* (Federer pp. 67-68)

At the ripe age of 75, he wrote to Rev. Haygood: *"...if we do not take Christ seriously in our every day life, all is a failure because it is an every day affair."* (Federer p. 84)   He once remarked: *"The secret of my success? It is simple. It is found in the Bible, 'In all thy ways acknowledge Him and He shall direct thy paths.'"* (Federer p. 86)

Carver said of his daily walk with the Lord: *"...all my life I have risen regularly at four o'clock and have gone into the woods and talked with God. There He gives me my orders for the day."* (Ferrell, p. 58) And he further proclaimed: *"How I thank God every day that I can walk and talk with Him."* (Federer p. 61)

We can *all* thank God that Carver walked and talked with the Lord, because we have all benefitted from that relationship.

Carver's ability to make seamless connections between his daily work and his faith is a model for us all. When it came to Carver's work, he was able to find God's pleasure in it because he knew God, and he knew what God's Word has to say about the meaning of work, the purpose of work, and what success in the work-world really looks like.

Because he knew God and His Word, Carver, like John Beckett, was able to make significant intentional connections between the truths of the Bible and his daily work in the lab.

This is the big challenge we all face: *making relevant and significant connections between the truths of God's Word and the everyday tasks of our daily work.* It's one thing to know what the Bible has to say in general terms, but it's another thing to apply it specifically to our daily work. But if every follower of Christ were to do this, as Carver did, and Beckett does, the world would be a much different place.

In light of this challenge and hope, I'd like to give you a tool which will help you make specific alignments between your faith and your daily work, as Carver's life example demonstrates. This tool is called, the "DADI Question."

"DADI" is an acronym that stands for *Discover, Apply, Develop,* and *Implement.* The DADI Question itself looks like this:

> *With respect to my work as a (plumber, etc.) what can I "DADI" (Discover, Apply, Develop, Implement) in connection with the biblical view of God, or Creation, or Humanity, or Moral Order or Purpose?*

As you can see, there is a blank to fill in. That's where you put whatever kind of work you do, or whatever particular aspect of your work you want to focus on. For example, if you are a plumber, you might fill in the blank with the word "plumber," or, if you happen to be a plumber who also submits bids on large construction jobs, you might want to focus on that particular aspect of your work and fill in the blank with something like, "bidder on large plumbing jobs."

If George Washington Carver was going to go through the DADI Question process, he would probably have filled in the blank with the word, "botanist," or possibly something like, "innovator of new products from plants."

The best way to learn how to use The DADI Question is to look at an example. With this in mind, I have answered The DADI Question as though I were George Washington Carver, based on what I know about the man from books written about his faith and his work. Understand, however, that my answers to The DADI Question, in this case, are only educated guesses.

First, let's look at The DADI Question with respect to how Carver connected his work with the biblical view of *God,* then we'll look at how he connected his work with the biblical view of *Creation,* then with the biblical view of *Humanity, Moral Order* and, finally, *Purpose.* First, here is The DADI Question as it relates to *God:*

> *With respect to my work as <u>an innovator of new products from plants</u> what can I "DADI" (Discover, Apply, Develop, Implement) in connection with the biblical view of GOD?*

Now, the **first task** is for Carver to figure out exactly *which aspect* of the biblical view of God he will focus upon. He writes this in the "DISCOVERY" section of the DADI process.

But there are hundreds of aspects of God he could choose from! The idea behind The DADI Question, however, is to *narrow* it down to one *specific* aspect of God that Carver has discovered from his study of the Bible which relates to his work with plants.

For the sake of illustration, I have imagined one aspect of God that Carver certainly had discovered from the Bible, and I have written this as an "I BELIEVE" statement in the "discovery" section of the DADI process, as follows:

"<u>I believe</u> God communicates with human beings about specific things, and He can give me understanding and wisdom about creating new things from plants, if I'm listening."

For followers of Christ like Carver, workplace values and behaviors are governed by biblical worldview beliefs that drive and guide those values and behavior. This is why we start the DADI process by articulating biblically-based belief in the "discovery" section of the DADI process.

I'm going through the DADI process in detail here, because it is my hope that each of you will go through the DADI process for yourself in the next chapter, in connection with how the biblical view of God, Creation, Humanity, Moral Order or Purpose relates to *your* work.

The **next step** in this process is to figure out how what is understood about God could be *applied* to your work, or in Carver's case, how it could be applied to his work as an innovator of new products from plants.

Again, for the sake of illustration, I have imagined how Carver might have *applied* his discovery about God to his work with plants, and I have written this as a visionary "I COULD" statement in the "apply" section of the DADI process, as follows:

"I could ask God why He made the peanut, and He could show me how to create new products from this plant."

The **third step** in the DADI process is to figure out what training, discipline, or preparation must take place in order to successfully fulfill the *I could* vision statement that was written in the "apply" section of the DADI process, as shown above. In Carter's case, I imagine he would have said something like the following, which has been written as an "I MUST" statement in the "develop" section of the DADI process:

"I must make prayer a part of my daily life, as well as a regular part of my work with plants in the lab. I must take time to listen to the Lord of all plants."

The **fourth and final step** in the DADI process is to determine specific action steps to be taken. In Carver's case, I imagine he would have said something like the following, which I have written as an "I WILL" statement in the "implement" section of the DADI process:

"I will rise at 4:00 am so I can talk with God and receive my orders for the day. I will ask the Great Creator why He made the peanut. I will lock the door of my lab so I can have a quiet place to hear His secrets."

To recap so far, there are four aspects to one's answer to The DADI Question, as illustrated above by Carter's answers I have provided, based on what I know about him. First of all, there is an *I believe statement* about what Carver discovered and believed to be true about *God* in relation to his work with plants, followed by a visionary *I could statement* about how this discovery became part of his daily work with plants, followed by an *I must statement* regarding the training, discipline, or preparation that was necessary to turn his vision into reality, and, finally an *I will statement* about specific action steps Carver took.

In the pages that follow, let's imagine how George Washington Carver would have answered The DADI Question with respect to how his work with plants related to the other four components of the biblical view: *Creation, Humanity, Moral Order* and *Purpose*. We'll use the same process we followed with respect to how Carver related his work to the biblical view of *God*.

With respect to my work as <u>an innovator of new products from plants</u>, what can I "DADI" (Discover, Apply, Develop, Implement) in connection with the biblical view of CREATION?

DISCOVER
(What biblical revelation about *Creation* relates to my work?)

<u>I believe</u> that after plants were created, humans were commissioned to rule over them as co-workers with God.

APPLY
(In what way could this revelation be a part of my work?)

<u>I could</u> rule over the peanut, the sweet potato and the soybean, by co-working with God to create new products from these plants.

DEVELOP
(What training, discipline or preparation must take place to bring this about?)

<u>I must</u> learn all I can about botany and chemistry in order to rule well over peanuts, sweet potatoes and soybeans in the lab.

IMPLEMENT
(What specific action steps will I take?)

<u>I will</u> spend time with God in 'His Little Workshop,' using my knowledge of botany and chemistry, taking apart plants and putting them together again as He shows me how to create new things.

With respect to my work as <u>an innovator of new products from plants</u>, what can I "DADI" (Discover, Apply, Develop, Implement) in connection with the biblical view of HUMANITY?

DISCOVER
(What biblical revelation about *Humanity* relates to my work?)

<u>I believe</u> humans are the highest embodiment of God's handiwork, and are to be loved most.

APPLY
(In what way could this revelation be a part of my work?)

I could demonstrate my love for farmers by teaching them about effective crop rotation and I could create products from these crops to generate new markets.

DEVELOP
(What training, discipline or preparation must take place to bring this about?)

I must develop a practical way of educating farmers about crop rotation. I must create new products for industrial uses from peanuts, sweet potatoes and soybeans.

IMPLEMENT
(What specific action steps will I take?)

I will create a "School on Wheels" to teach farmers. With God's help, I will create industrial uses for the peanut, sweet potato and soybean, and encourage new markets for farmers.

With respect to my work as an innovator of new products from plants, what can I "DADI" (Discover, Apply, Develop, Implement) in connection with the biblical view of MORAL ORDER?

DISCOVER
(What biblical revelation about *Moral Order* relates to my work?)

I believe humans have a responsibility to manage God's creation in ways that are resourceful and beneficial, without waste or abuse.

APPLY
(In what way could this revelation be a part of my work?)

I could find uses for the renewable resource of the peanut, the sweet potato and the soybean, benefiting people and industry yet being kind to the land at the same time.

DEVELOP
(What training, discipline or preparation must take place to bring this about?)

I must do all I can to encourage applied research in crop rotation, creating new products from plants, and encouraging the use of such crops in industry.

IMPLEMENT
(What specific action steps will I take?)

I will establish a center for the development of renewable plant resources for industry. I will develop relationships with leaders in industry, such as Henry Ford, to encourage use of such resources.

With respect to my work as _an innovator of new products from plants,_ what can I "DADI" (Discover, Apply, Develop, Implement) in connection with the biblical view of PURPOSE?

DISCOVER
(What biblical revelation about *Purpose* relates to my work?)

I believe living for others is really what the Christ life is all about.

APPLY
(In what way could this revelation be a part of my work?)

I could use my skills as a botanist and a chemist to produce beneficial products that will serve farmers and better their lives.

DEVELOP
(What training, discipline or preparation must take place to bring this about?)

I must work hard to combine my knowledge of botany and chemistry with my trust in God to create industrial products from plants that will truly help farmers find new markets.

IMPLEMENT
(What specific action steps will I take?)

I will create new products from plants, and establish a Center for Research at Tuskegee Institute that will continue long after I am gone.

Carver had his priorities straight. He was a man who saw the hand of God at work in the world, and he did what he could to come alongside Him in that work. Carver co-labored with the Great Creator, and in the process he succeeded at seamlessly integrating his faith with his work in such a way that God was honored, the Lord was pleased, and humans were blessed.

Carver's story should cause us to marvel, not just at his ingenuity and scientific prowess, but at the amazing creativity which came to him as he laid aside his own ego and gave an attentive ear to what God revealed to him in the laboratory, and even in his sleep.

In the next chapter, we'll continue our focus on The DADI Question, as we look at a more recent example from the world of scientific discovery, examining the work of Gary Starkweather, inventor of the laser printer.

Talking Point: What other examples (past or present) can you give of people who have been able to "live seamlessly" as followers of Christ in the world, without compartmentalizing their lives into so-called "sacred" and "secular" boxes?

Do you think "living seamlessly" as a follower of Christ in the work-world was easier in Carver's day than it is today? Why or why not?

Chapter Eight

Personalizing the DADI Question

Gary Starkweather worked for Hewlett Packard when he invented the laser printer, and he later worked as a developer of new technologies for Microsoft at its Redmond, Washington headquarters, not far from our home.

My wife, Kathy, and I got to know Gary and his wife, Joyce, when we attended the same church for several years, during which time Gary taught a Sunday adult Bible class that we attended. Like George Washington Carver, Gary has a love for the Scriptures. Carver, too, held a regular Bible class for students at Tuskegee Institute for many years, on Sunday evenings, and continued this practice after he retired from his teaching and research duties.

Realizing that Gary Starkweather had a well-developed biblical worldview, I asked him for a video interview at the Microsoft lab, and he kindly obliged.

I'll never forget this experience, as we met on a Saturday morning at the Microsoft lab, when all the other workers were gone. Entering the lab was like coming onto the set of "The Bride of Frankenstein" film. The only thing missing was Igor and the arching electricity. A large whiteboard full of mathematical scribbling provided the perfect backdrop, and I asked Gary to sit in front of it as I did the interview.

As you watch this interview, listen for how Gary has discovered, applied, developed and implemented the biblical view of God, Creation, Humanity, Moral Order and Purpose with respect to his work as a developer of new technology. Listen for biblical worldview premises that drive and guide his workplace values and behavior.

Before you watch, let me explain that during part of this interview you will see a computer screen Gary invented (called the "D-Sharp" screen) that appears to be undulating. It is not. The illusion was caused by the frame speed of my video camera.

DVD Clip #16
Gary Starkweather: Inventor of the Laser Printer
Approx. 6 minutes

Hopefully you caught many connections between Gary's biblical worldview and his work in the field of technology. In case some biblical worldview premises went by quickly, here are a few to consider:

"Since He made us in His image, the creativity we possess is there because the Creator put it there."

"God put things in us as tool developers and creative individuals, and it pleases Him when He sees us use those faculties to make something completely new."

"When we use the skills God gave us, it can't help but give Him pleasure, and hence we feel that pleasure in us: 'You're using what I built in you!'"

Somewhere along the way, Gary Starkweather learned to experience God's pleasure at work. Based on the content of this interview, I put together a DADI Question response that reflects Gary's thought process as it relates to the biblical view of *Purpose.* The DADI Question, in this case, becomes: *"With respect to my work as <u>an innovator of new technologies</u>, what can I discover, apply, develop and implement in connection with the biblical view of Purpose?"*

Below are some answers, based on what I know about Gary Starkweather and his biblical view of work and *Purpose:*

DISCOVER
(What biblical revelation about *Purpose* relates to my work?)

I believe God created all humans in His image, and therefore there is something special about each one of us that we ought to try and cultivate, and ask God, "What is this unique quality that I ought to really make work for You?"

APPLY
(In what way could this revelation be a part of my work?)

I could put the gifts God has given me to work by taking ideas and turning them into tangible realities in the field of computer technology and optics.

DEVELOP
(What training, discipline or preparation must take place to bring this about?)

I must be very knowledgeable about optics. I must learn to compete in the open market. If my faith is really what I say it is, then I ought to excel in fields where those who do not have my faith are playing.

IMPLEMENT
(What specific action steps will I take?)

I will devote myself to co-working with God to create new things (such as the laser printer and the D-Sharp screen) that will benefit the human race in the 21st Century.

Now that you've seen examples of the DADI Question applied to the work of Carver, and one example of how it applied to the work of Gary Starkweather, it's time to try your hand at it. It is a process that can be applied to *any* kind of work, at any level of responsibility. It doesn't just apply to the work of inventors. It applies to your work, too.

The process is straightforward, but it isn't the kind of thing you can do quickly, or without some prayerful reflection. It is also something you probably won't do in a group setting. I recommend that you work on this by yourself, and then bring your completed DADI Question to share with your group.

Allow me to walk you through the four-step DADI process with a few words of instruction.

Step 1: In the "Discover" section of the DADI process, try to think of one *specific* biblical truth about God, or Creation, or Humanity, or Moral Order, or Purpose that has *particular relevance to your work*, or to a certain aspect of your work.

This process is not easy, but it isn't rocket science either. It requires some knowledge of what the Bible has to say about the five areas of every worldview (God, Creation, Humanity, Moral Order and Purpose), and it requires some thoughtful consideration as to how the one specific biblical truth you pick has particular relevance to your work.

To get your creative juices going, you may want to go to the back of this book (see the Appendix), where you will find a list of 50 specific biblical truths that relate to the workplace, arranged in groupings that correspond to the five worldview components. While it is a generic list, this collection may spark some specific ideas in your mind.

The goal of the "Discover" section of the DADI process is to narrow your thinking to *one* biblical truth, and write that biblical premise in the "Discover" area shown on the next page. Your statement is an "I BELIEVE" statement. Remember, it is from this biblical starting point that the rest of the DADI process flows.

Step 2: In the "Apply" section of the DADI process, take some time to ask God for a *compelling vision*. Ask Him for specific ideas on how you can apply what you have written in the "Discover" box to your own work situation. Feel free to "draw outside the lines" here. Go back and read the examples from the George Washington Carver chapter (Chapter 7). If it will help, talk it over with a friend. Give it some time. Pray about it. Sleep on it.

The main idea here is to "flesh out" what you really believe to be true with respect to the biblical worldview, in a way that has genuine and relevant connections with some aspect of the work you do. Being specific is important here.

Step 3: In the "Develop" section of the DADI process, think about what you may need to do in order to be successful in making the vision that you have articulated in Step 2 a reality. For example, you might want to take some classes or read some books related to what you want to do. You may want to talk with some experts. You may want to do some research, or you may want to fast and pray.

Step 4: In the "Implement" section of the DADI process, write out your specific action steps.

DISCOVER: *I believe*

APPLY: *I could*

DEVELOP: *I must*

IMPLEMENT: *I will*

Talking Point: Do you feel you are truly using your God-given gifts at work? Are you truly sensing God's pleasure in your use of those gifts at work?

As Gary Starkweather said, "When we use the skills God gave us, it can't help but give Him pleasure, and hence we feel that pleasure in us: 'You're using what I built in you!'"

No matter how experienced you may be in making connections between your faith and your work, I trust that by going through the DADI process you have made new connections that you may never have considered before.

The DADI exercise is neither a one-time exercise, nor a quick-fix, but rather a process of continually returning to God's Word and challenging ourselves to align our work with His Word to a greater and greater degree.

I urge you to share your DADI plan with your group. I also recommend that you pencil into your calendar periodic times to share progress with your group, or with a close friend, over the next few months and beyond.*

*If you are willing to share your DADI plan with others around the world for the purpose of mutual assistance and idea-sharing, you may send your DADI plan to Worldview Matters at info@worldviewmatters.com, where it will be considered for inclusion with other DADI plans open for viewing on the Worldview Matters website (www.worldviewmatters.com). Worldview Matters cannot guarantee that all DADI plans received will be published on the site, nor can we provide feedback on DADI plans submitted.

Chapter Nine

"But Doesn't the Bible Say...?"

Perhaps during this course you've thought to yourself, "This all sounds interesting, but doesn't the Bible say, 'Set your mind on things above, *not* on things on the earth?' And doesn't the Bible say, 'Do *not* love the world or the *things in the world?'*"

If these verses have come to your mind, I applaud your knowledge of Scripture and your inquiring mind. As followers of Christ, we are responsible for filtering everything we read and hear through the grid of the Word of God. So with that in mind, let's take a closer look at these verses.

Col. 3:2 clearly states: *Set your mind on things above, not on things on the earth.* But if you look at the context of this verse, taking it from verse 1 to verse 15, you will discover that what Paul has in mind when he speaks of the "things on the earth" is not your house, your car, or your lawnmower. And it's not your checking account or your job. Please read verses 1-15:

If then you were raised with Christ, seek those things which are above, where Christ is, sitting at the right hand of God. Set your mind on things above, not on things on the earth. For you died, and your life is hidden with Christ in God. When Christ who is our life appears, then you also will appear with Him in glory. Therefore put to death your members which are on the earth: fornication, uncleanness, passion, evil desire, and covetousness, which is idolatry. Because of these things the wrath of God is coming upon the sons of disobedience, in which you yourselves once walked when you lived in them. But now you yourselves are to put off all these: anger, wrath, malice, blasphemy, filthy language out of your mouth. Do not lie to one another, since you have put off the old man with his deeds, and have put on the new man who is renewed in knowledge according to the image of Him who created him, where there is neither Greek nor Jew, circumcised nor uncir-

cumcised, barbarian, Scythian, slave nor free, but Christ is all and in all. Therefore, as the elect of God, holy and beloved, put on tender mercies, kindness, humility, meekness, longsuffering; bearing with one another, and forgiving one another, if anyone has a complaint against another; even as Christ forgave you, so you also must do. But above all these things put on love, which is the bond of perfection. And let the peace of God rule in your hearts, to which also you were called in one body; and be thankful. [New King James Version]

So when Paul writes, "set your mind on things above," the context leads to this conclusion: "Set your mind on tender mercies, kindness, humility, meekness, longsuffering, bearing with one another, forgiving one another, love, peace, and thankfulness." And when Paul says, "Don't set your mind on things on the earth," he is actually saying, "Don't set your mind on fornication, uncleanness, passion, evil desire, covetousness, anger, wrath, malice, blasphemy, filthy language, and lies."

So when you sing that old chorus, "Turn your eyes upon Jesus, look full in His wonderful face, and the things of earth will grow strangely dim...," I hope your front lawn that needs mowing isn't fading in your mind, or your house that needs painting, or your bank account, or the work that is waiting for you at the office.

What's very interesting about Colossians 3 is the fact that in this *same* chapter Paul pens some of the most significant words in the New Testament that relate directly to the matter of work: "*...do your work heartily, as for the Lord rather than for men...*" (verse 23). Clearly, Paul is not suggesting that followers of Christ quit taking their work seriously. Just the opposite!

Talking Point: Is the understanding of Col. 3:2 as explained above a different understanding than you previously had? Will this understanding make any difference in your thinking about work?

DO NOT LOVE THE WORLD

Then there's that verse in I John 2, which states: "*Do not love the world or the things that are in the world*" (verse 15, NKJV). To understand what John is intending, we need to realize that the English word *world,* translated from the Greek word *kosmos* in the New Testament, has four meanings in Scripture.

First, the word *world* can refer to "populated regions," as in Romans 1:8: *I thank my God through Jesus Christ for you all, that your faith is spoken of throughout the whole world [kosmos].*

Second, the word *world* can refer to "the human race" in general, as in John 3:16: *For God so loved the world [kosmos] that He gave His only begotten Son, that whosoever believes in Him should not perish, but have everlasting life.* Obviously, if we take the word *world* in I John 2:15 to mean "the human race,"then we have a very big problem, because *God* loves the *world* [that is, the human race], and we are also commanded to love the human race.

Third, the word *world* can refer to "the created realm," as in Romans 1:20: *For since the creation of the world [kosmos] His invisible attributes are clearly seen, being understood by the things that are made, even His eternal power and Godhead, so that they are without excuse...*

Fourth, the word *world* can refer to "a system of thought and behavior that is contrary to the will and ways of God," as in Colossians 2:8: *Beware lest anyone cheat you through philosophy and empty deceit, according to the tradition of men, according to the basic principles of the world [kosmos], and not according to Christ.*

So let's go back to I John 2:15 and take a closer look, along with the two verses immediately following it (v. 16-17): *Do not love the world [kosmos], or the things in the world [kosmos]. If anyone loves the world [kosmos], the love of the Father is not in him. For all that is in the world [kosmos] — the lust of the flesh, the lust of the eyes, and the pride of life — is not of the Father but is of the world [kosmos].*

Verse 17 actually clarifies what John is talking about when he uses the word *world* in verse 15. John is telling us not to love the world system of thought and behavior that is contrary to the will and ways of God, which is governed by the lust of the flesh, the lust of the eyes, and the pride of life.

Below are other verses in which the word *world* seems to have the meaning of "the world-system," as described above:

John 8:23: *And He [Jesus] said to them [the religious leaders], "You are from beneath; I am from above. You are of this world (system); I am not of this world (system)."*

John 17:14-18 is very interesting because in this short passage we find several different meanings of the word *world*: *"I do not pray that You should take [My disciples] out of the world [the created realm], but that You should keep them from the evil one. They are not of the world [system], just as I am not of the world [system]...As You sent Me into the world [populated regions, or the created realm], I also have sent them into the world [populated regions, or the created realm]."*

Eph. 2:1-3 says: *And you He made alive, who were dead in trespasses and sins, in which you once walked according to the course of this world (system), according to the prince of the power of the air, the spirit who now works in the sons of disobedience...*

The "prince of the power of the air" is a reference to Satan, who was cast from heaven to earth, where he currently roams around "like a roaring lion, seeking whom he may devour."

In John 12:31, 14:30 and 16:11, Jesus refers to Satan as *"the ruler of this world [kosmos]."* The question now becomes, *which* meaning of the word *world* is Jesus using when He refers to Satan as the "ruler of this *world?"* If we take this verse to mean that Satan is the ruler of the realm of creation, or the ruler of the populated regions of the globe, or the ruler of the human race in general, then we have a problem with other verses that clearly declare Jesus is Lord of all (Acts 19:36), and that His kingdom is over all (I Chron. 29:11, Daniel 4:32), and that the earth is the Lord's "and all it contains" (Psalm 24:1).

Although Satan is not the ruler of planet Earth, he *is* ruler of the *world-system* that is opposed to the will and ways of God. Although he *acts* like he is the ruler of planet Earth, and he would have us believe he is, such is not the case.

Some readers might be wondering about the temptation of Christ in Luke 4, where Satan took Jesus to the top of a high mountain and offered Him all the "kingdoms *of the world.*"

Which meaning of the word *world* fits best here? If Satan was offering Jesus all the kingdoms of the realm of creation, or the populated regions of humankind, it was a bogus offer, because this belongs to the Lord, and is not Satan's to give away. (Of course, Satan is the master of bogus offers.)

Luke 4:5 says: *Then the devil, taking Him up on a high mountain, showed Him all the kingdoms of the world in a moment of time.* [By the way, the word "world" here is not *kosmos*. It is *oikoumene*, which is translated "earth," or "world."]

What exactly was Satan showing Jesus? Was he showing Him the skyline of ancient Rome? Or did he go forward in time and show Jesus the skyscrapers of Manhattan or Tokyo?

Or, could Satan have been showing Jesus something else? Could Satan have been showing Christ the hosts of fallen angels that are referred to in the Bible as "principalities and powers of the air?" It seems a mountain top would be a fitting place to put on such a display.

I can't say for sure, but I think it is possible that Satan was showing Christ a vast display of demons, rather than a panoramic view of real estate. I say this because of the verse that follows, in which Satan says: "All this *authority* I will give You, and their glory; for this has been delivered to me, and I give it to whomever I wish."

Is it possible that Satan was tempting Jesus with the power to once again have at His disposal all the angelic creatures who at one time served God in Heaven but now serve Satan on Earth? Jesus could have them back, if only He would bow down and worship the devil. "If you will worship before me," Satan declared, "all will be yours!"

Jesus' response was: "Get behind me Satan! For it is written, 'You shall worship the Lord your God, and Him only you shall serve.'" And with this rebuke, the temptation was over.

Why have I taken space to mention all this about Satan? I've done so because some people have assumed that planet Earth belongs to Satan, when in fact it belongs to God. Some have assumed that when Adam and Eve fell, they lost their job as vice-regents of God, and that God has withdrawn the First

Commission that He gave to humans, as co-rulers over the Blue Planet.

If we make these assumptions, there may be a tendency to think more about Heaven than Earth, with respect to our current role of responsibility as co-workers with God in it. If we accept these notions, they can have a profoundly negative effect upon our view of work, and our view of the material world itself. These faulty assumptions may hold us back from fully engaging with the material world of the here-and-now with the kind of abandon, vigor and enthusiasm befitting a co-worker with the Creator. This is who we are.

Talking Point: What are the implications of this chapter for followers of Christ in workplaces in general, and for you in your workplace in particular?

Chapter Ten

The ATII Question

So far, we've looked at work in the fields of business, agriculture, the arts, and technology. In this chapter, I'd like to focus on education, because education has such a profound effect upon the culture at large, and on the state of the workplace in general.

Much of my personal work over the years has been with school teachers, helping them to make connections between academic subject matter and the bigger picture of a biblical worldview. For fourteen years I was principal of a Christian school where we endeavored to integrate faith with learning in practical ways.

Since the year 2000, I have worked with The Biblical Worldview Institute, a division of Cascade Christian Schools in Puyallup, Washington, assisting with the development of effective ways to incorporate the biblical worldview into academic lesson plans. One of the tools we developed at The Institute is a course that trains school teachers in how to make the connections between every academic subject and the bigger picture of a biblical worldview. This course is titled, *Making the Connections.* (If you are a school teacher and you want more information, please visit www.biblicalworldviewinstitute.org.)

I have had the privilege of teaching the *Making the Connections* course across the USA, as well as in Central America, Europe, Africa and Asia. Occasionally I have been asked, "Do you teach this course for public school teachers?" My answer is always the same: "Well, I *would* teach it, but I don't receive many invitations from public schools."

However, I did receive one such invitation from a public school superintendent who had oversight of a district with 16,000 students, in a city of 125,000 people.

I was surprised to receive this invitation. I asked if I could meet with this superintendent, because I wanted to share specifically what the *Making the Connections* course was about. Frankly, I was concerned he might lose his job if I were to come teach this course. The course is very straightforward in its presentation of the Bible as the foundation for the methodology, and I do not hesitate in this regard when I teach it.

So we met together for three hours at the superintendent's downtown office. As I shared with him what *Making the Connections* was all about, he made this remarkable statement: "Teaching Christianity to the students is more important to me than academics." When he said this, I realized this man knew full well what he wanted. So I agreed to come and teach the course.

What I haven't mentioned, is this school district is not in America. It's in Ukraine, a former satellite of the Soviet Union. The town is Uzhgorod, in the far western region, near the Slovakian and Hungarian borders.

I spent three days with about twenty vice-principals of the Uzhgorod public school system who were charged with implementing a Christian-based moral education curriculum which the superintendent had already introduced into the school district.

While in Uzhgorod, I was invited to visit one of the K-8 schools with my interpreter, Anya Moisei. I have to tell you, what I saw and heard there blew my mind. A friend of mine, Jim Park, came along with a video camera, and recorded my visit. I'd like you to view my visit.

DVD Clip #17
Public School Visit
Approx. 4 minutes

Talking Point: What do you think about what I saw in this Ukrainian public school? What was going through your mind when you heard the students respond to my questions?

The question in the minds of many American Christians who watch this video is: *"What happened to our educational system here in the United States?"*

What *did* happen?

Like the Soviet Union, the United States also had a revolution in the 20th Century. However, the American revolution was the quiet, slow type. Allow me to explain.

There are two basic routes to societal change: loud and fast, or quiet and slow. Russia, in the Revolution of 1917, took the loud and fast route. Shots were fired, people were killed, change was sudden, and vocal Christians were taken to prison by force. The eventual reversal, some seventy years later, came rather suddenly as well.

America took the slow route, in the quiet revolution of 1859-1962. No shots were fired. No people were killed. Change spanned several generations. People didn't realize they were taken captive until after the fact, because they were allowed to live in their homes and send their children to the neighborhood schools as though nothing was happening at all. We were taken captive through *ideas*, and because of this, a reversal is not likely to be sudden.

Because it took several generations of "ramping up" to lay a foundation for the pivotal decade of the 60s, it may take that amount of time to ramp up to a reversal. I hope not, but I don't think it's going to be a "quick fix." We who live in the "instant age" must learn to take a long-range, generational approach to the reversal process.

1859

Let's take a closer look at the quiet American revolution of 1859-1962. The exact dates are hard to pin down, but I have selected 1859 as a starting point because this was the year that Charles Darwin came out with *The Origin of Species*.

It is not much of a stretch to say that Charles Darwin had more influence on the course of 20th Century history than any other human being. Darwin had as much influence on the loud and fast Russian revolution of 1917 as he did on the quiet and slow American revolution of 1859-1962.

Darwin's book on *Origins* probably had more effect upon the course of American (and Western European) history than any other book besides the Bible. This is because Darwin's book gave people a seemingly scientific and respectable basis for belief in the worldview of Naturalism (the idea that *Nature* is all there is, or was, or ever will be), and a basis for eventually removing any serious consideration of a Creator from public instruction.*

On the heels of Darwin, the most influential person in the course of American public education in the 20th Century was certainly John Dewey.

Dewey was a committed atheist, and one of the signers of the first Humanist Manifesto of 1933. Ironically, John Dewey was born in 1859, the year Darwin's *Origins* came into print. He lived a long life, having passed on to meet his Creator in 1952.

Dewey was a world-class philosopher who earned the title, Father of Progressive Education. He taught education courses at Columbia University Teachers College, in New York City, and he saw education as the primary venue for affecting social change. He realized that his Darwinian worldview was a *faith* that could find free expression in American elementary and secondary schools. Yes, Dewey referred to his non-theistic worldview as a "faith," and he was correct to do so.

Talking Point: What does this discussion about Charles Darwin and John Dewey have to do with today's workplace? What role does the education of children play in shaping the culture of tomorrow's workplaces?

*I say Darwin's book provided a "seemingly" scientific basis for evolution, because his theory of evolution is not very scientific. This may sound like an audacious statement coming from someone who is not a scientist. But today, some highly qualified scientists are speaking out about this matter. Most are keeping quiet because to be anti-Darwin is a sure way to lose funding. Some of these scientists who don't accept Darwin's theory are not Christians, and they have no God-centered agenda. One scientist who is speaking out is Dr. David Berlinski, a former Post Doctoral Fellow in molecular biology at Columbia University who holds a Ph. D. in philosophy from Princeton. An interview with him, called, "The Incorrigible Dr. Berlinski" is available from Coldwater Media, 719-488-8670, or, www.coldwatermedia.com.

Dewey's faith held that the universe is self-existing and not created. It is therefore not surprising that he proclaimed: *"...the time has passed for belief in theism..."*, and: *"we consider the religious forms and ideas of our fathers no longer adequate..."*

If you think American public schools are religiously neutral, *think again.* They are definitely faith-based. Humanism is a very religious worldview indeed. It is a *non-theistic faith.* Furthermore, it has been the undeclared official faith of American public schools for quite some time now. And if you don't think this is affecting today's workplace, think again (again).

This matter of not mixing religion with our public schools today is an issue which needs to be carefully re-examined. The question is not whether religion will be allowed to mix with education, but *which* religion will be allowed to mix. The fact of the matter is, religion *is* being mixed with our public schools today. It's just a *different* religion than the one that was mixed with education in the days of the Founding Fathers, such as Noah Webster.

Consider this: if it is *not* allowable to teach that the world was created by God, and yet it *is* allowable to teach that the world came into being on its own, is it not equally a faith position to teach that God did *not* create the world, as it is to teach that He *did?* If it is a *religious* statement to say, "God created the world," is it not also a *religious* statement to say, "God did not create the world"? Think about it. Are not *both* of these statements religious positions, taken by faith?

To declare to children that "God did not create the world" can be done very effectively without actually saying those specific words. A teacher does not have to stand up in front of a class and tell them that the biblical account of creation is a fable in order to communicate the idea it is fiction.

Consider this: if it is *not* allowable to teach children that God has spoken to mankind through the Bible and that His Word is an absolute moral standard for us all, and yet it *is* allowable to teach them that morality is something determined by society itself and is relative to society's own desires and ideals, then is it not *equally* a position of *faith* to teach that God's Word is *not* the moral standard for man as it is to teach that it *is?* If it is a religious statement to say, "The Bible is man's ultimate standard of morality," is it not also a religious statement to say, in so many words or lack thereof, "The Bible is *not* man's ultimate standard of morality"?

Talking Point: Do you agree or disagree with these last three paragraphs? What difference does it make for the workplace?

All schools that have a stated mission and purpose are faith-based, just as all churches are. It can be no other way, for behind all missions and purposes are ideologies, and all ideologies are based on certain assumptions which can only be accepted by faith.

It takes faith to believe that God created life, and it takes faith to believe that life came from non-life. (A great deal of faith, indeed!) It takes faith to believe that the Bible is a book of moral absolutes, and it takes faith to believe that man is "the measure of all things," as one Greek philosopher put it.

It is impossible to divorce education, government, or any other sphere of life from faith assumptions of one sort or another. And furthermore, *somebody's* faith will end up being the ultimate guiding factor in any of these spheres of life, be it in the classroom, the pulpit, or the workplace.

But we can't pin the whole quiet American revolution on Darwin and Dewey. They were just two individuals. But individuals *do* make a difference, and these two men were key individuals in turning education in a direction Noah Webster could not have imagined when America was founded. Once this was accomplished, however, it was only a matter of time before students of one generation became teachers of the next. And so the quiet revolution rolled on.

I selected 1962 as the date of the other bracket of the quiet American revolution because this was the year the U.S. Supreme Court determined it was unconstitutional for public school personnel to lead students in prayer. The rest of the changes came quickly after that. The process leading up to this state of affairs took 103 years.

LOOKING IT SQUARE IN THE FACE

It's not just our kids who are facing alien philosophies that are "according to the traditions of men and not according to Christ." What is true in the realm of education is also true in the business world, the media, the arts and sciences, and in every other field of endeavor.

Neither we nor our children can afford to continue to be taken captive by the vain philosophies that are pressing in on us from all sides. We must not only help our children, but we must take active steps ourselves, as adults, to keep from being taken captive by ideas that are alien to Christ.

We can choose to turn our heads, or we can look the alien ideas square in the face, and engage them head-on. With this in mind, I want to give you a powerful mental tool that will help you (and your children, if you have any) not to be *taken* captive, but rather to *take* thoughts captive to the obedience of Christ. (Compare Col. 3:8 with I Cor. 10:4.) The tool is called called, *the ATII Question.*

"ATII" is an acronym for "Assumed, Taught, Ignored or Implied." The ATII Question goes like this:

"With respect to _______________________, what is being ATII'd (Assumed, Taught, Ignored or Implied) about God, Creation, Humanity, Moral Order or Purpose?"

As we saw with the DADI Question, the ATII Question has a blank to be filled in by you. I'm going to fill it in with a sample, so you will get the idea of how the ATII Question works. In this case, I'm going to use an example from a children's television program, called *Reading Rainbow.* Specifically, I'm going to fill the blank in with *Reading Rainbow Episode #129: Giving Thanks.*

The basic idea behind the ATII Question is to compare and contrast worldview beliefs contained in media, film, books, and any other form of communication that comes your way. When I say "compare and contrast," I'm referring to comparing and contrasting various worldview beliefs that come our way with the worldview we understand to be true from the Bible.

The process is rather straightforward, but I can't say it is easy. The grid below gives you the overall picture.

	GOD	*CREATION*	*HUMANITY*	*MORAL ORDER*	*PURPOSE*
Assumed					
Taught					
Ignored					
Implied					

Perhaps the best way to learn how to use the ATII Question is to use it to analyze the *Reading Rainbow* episode seen in the next DVD clip. We have edited this episode, but there is sufficient material here to get started with the ATII Question.

As you watch the DVD, consider what is being *Assumed, Taught, Ignored* or *Implied* about God, Creation, Humanity, Moral Order or Purpose. It would be very difficult to analyze this DVD with all five worldview components in mind. Rather, it is easier to focus on just one or two worldview components. You might want to transfer the above grid to a larger piece of paper so you can have more room to write notes in the respective squares.

If you are watching this DVD in a group, have some people watch for what is being Assumed, Taught, Ignored or Implied about *God,* and have others watch for what is being Assumed, Taught, Ignored or Implied about *Creation.* Have others watch with respect to the other worldview components of Humanity, Moral Order or Purpose.

As you watch, think about what is being ATTI'd that is in *harmony* with the biblical worldview as well as what is not. You will see both.

DVD Clip #18
Reading Rainbow Episode #129
Approx. 3 minutes

Talking Point: What did you see in Episode #129 that was being ATII'd (Assumed, Taught, Ignored or Implied) about God, Creation, Humanity, Moral Order or Purpose? What was in *harmony* with the biblical worldview? What was in *conflict* with the biblical worldview?

Yes, it is *good* to give thanks, and this is an important aspect of the biblical view of God and of Moral Order. Yes, farming is honorable and physical labor is good. Yes, humans are responsible to care for the environment. But things "went south" in this episode of *Reading Rainbow* in many respects.

NOT JUST FOR TV SHOWS

The ATII Question is a great tool to use when trying to assess *any* input coming your way, whether via company policy, ideas from co-workers, or input from customers. It can be used to evaluate business proposals. It can also be helpful when trying to organize your thoughts for board meetings, or giving presentations.

Of course, you don't have to let people know how you arrived at your ideas. It isn't necessary to label your ideas as "biblical," nor is it recommended, unless you are working in an environment where making intentional alignments with the biblical worldview is a shared objective.

If you have children, teach them to use the ATII Question. Go to a film together and go through the ATII process over ice cream afterwards. Teach them these analytical thinking skills. You'll be glad you took the time. If you are a school teacher, incorporate the ATII Question into your teaching, and help your students to learn to *take* thoughts captive, rather than *be taken* captive by them.

Chapter Eleven

Four Wheels of Work

If you walked out your front door one morning to go to work and discovered a wheel was missing from your car, what would you do? Would you replace it yourself? Would you have your car towed to a shop? Or would you just ignore the fact that a wheel is missing and try to drive to work anyway?

If you ignored the missing wheel and began driving, you would do considerable damage to your car, not to mention the possibility of bodily damage to yourself or others.

The title of this chapter is "Four Wheels of Work." The main idea behind this chapter is that there are four "wheels of work" in our lives, and, just as with our car, all four are necessary to balance our overall work experience and provide the full benefits God intends for us through this marvelous thing called *work*.

While our occupations are one sphere of work, the three others are: our homes, our churches, and our communities.

We have been focusing mainly on the occupational wheel of work, and it is my hope that everyone will come out of the GPAW course with a greater passion for integrating their faith with their occupation. But there is a danger here. If we place too much emphasis on our occupations, we'll soon find we're omitting the other three wheels of work because we are just too busy focusing on one.

The fact is, some people need to focus on their occupations *less.* It is possible to spend too much time at the office, or to make one's occupation more of a focus than the Lord intends. When this happens, we may be putting our occupations above God. Yes, we are to worship God in and through our work, but we are not to worship our work *itself.* This is what the Bible calls "idolatry," and we'll never experience God's pleasure in this.

It would be tragic if people who went through GPAW came away with an unbalanced focus on their occupations to the neglect of their homes. Some readers may need to focus more on experiencing God's pleasure at work around the house. Getting the "honey-do" jobs done is also a way of working "as unto the Lord." If you haven't done so already, try mowing your lawn and washing the dishes as an act of worship, presenting your body a living sacrifice, holy and acceptable to God. Frustration diminishes, and peace increases.

And then there is the matter of rearing children and bringing them up "in the training and admonition of the Lord" (Eph. 6:4 NKJV). Talk about work! And, husbands, there's that equally no-small-matter of loving our wives "just as Christ also loved the church and gave Himself for her" (Eph. 5:25 NKJV). This can make our occupational jobs look like a cake walk! And, wives, respecting husbands can require some effort, too (Eph. 5:33). Having a healthy marriage requires work.

All of the concepts we've been talking about apply as much to work at home as they do to work at the office or the shop. If you are a stay-at-home parent, I hope you've been thinking about this all along. If you haven't, I suggest perhaps you go through the course again with your work at home in mind.

Talking Point: Exactly how do the concepts we've been talking about in this course apply to the "honey do" jobs around the house, to child rearing and to marriage? Be specific.

CONNECTING WITH THE MISSION OF YOUR LOCAL CHURCH OR PARISH
The third wheel is our work with our local church or parish. It would be absurd to say, "I don't need to lift a helping hand at church because I'm already worshipping the Lord through mowing my lawn, loving my wife, and working at the shop five days a week!"

But one of the complaints some people have is that the work they are asked to do for the local church is not the most effective use of the gifts or strengths they could offer. While some CEOs may find passing the offering plate a welcome change from their week-day activity, others will be more fulfilled if their strengths are engaged in a challenging way.

Here's a suggestion: instead of waiting to be asked to serve as an usher (although this may be the perfect place for you), consider how you could blend your skills, strengths or interests with your local church's mission and vision, and come to the church leadership with a proposal.

Many churches these days have a mission/vision statement. If your local church or parish doesn't have one, make an appointment with your pastor or priest to find out what the mission and vision is for your congregation. In fact, even if your church or parish does have a mission/vision statement, it would be a good idea to meet together to find out more about what your leadership sees as God's direction for your particular congregation. Explain why you are asking, and see if your pastor or priest has some thoughts about how your strengths might best be used to further the Lord's mission and vision for your congregation.

Once you have clarity about your church's mission and vision, spend some time with the Lord, thinking and praying about how your skills and strengths might be most helpful. If married, invite your spouse (or perhaps your children) into the conversation. Maybe there would be a way to incorporate your entire family into service, thereby building not only your local church, but your own household.

Then come back to your pastor, priest, or appropriate staff member, with a proposal that best fits your strengths and available time commitment. Why wait for your church leaders to come to you? But remember, it's a proposal, not "baked bread." Be humbly open to further input and direction.

I'm not suggesting that you necessarily find a way to blend your *occupation* with your church's mission and vision, although this might be appropriate in many cases. My father was a mortician by occupation. The direct application of his vocational work in the church we attended was not a good fit. But Dad's love for fixing things and putting in new tile floors, led to work at the church that was helpful in keeping the buildings in good condition. And his gift for record keeping led to other types of helpful service.

In some cases, however, a direct blending of a person's occupation with the mission and vision of the local church might prove to be a perfect fit. If you are a professional chef who gets energized by cooking for groups, then preparing breakfast for the quarterly Saturday morning men's meeting might be a blessing to all concerned.

If you are a doctor who runs a medical clinic, and part of the mission and vision of your church is to provide practical care for low income families, perhaps some coordinated efforts between your clinic and the local church could be arranged. Or, if you are a lawyer, a similar arrangement with your church could be made in providing legal assistance for needy individuals. If you are an auto mechanic, concider donating some time to keep widows' cars running.

Talking Point: Does your occupation lend itself to an application in volunteer service for your local church or parish? If so, how?

Finding such ways to blend your occupational work with your church's mission and vision can be a great way to economize your personal time and energy. It can also be a way to engage with the fourth wheel of work: *the broader community.*

ENGAGING WITH THE BROADER COMMUNITY

In a very real sense, most people who work in an occupational capacity are also engaged with the fourth wheel of work at the same time, assuming their work takes place within the community. The occupations mentioned above are good examples. Communities need cooks, doctors, and mechanics. But communities also have needs that go unmet, for various reasons, and all communities have under-served areas that call for volunteer work to be done.

Community volunteerism is a great way for followers of Christ to "let our light so shine before men that they may see our good works and glorify our Father in heaven" (Matthew 5:16). It's also a great way for churches to channel the energies of willing workers in the congregation toward blessing those outside the four walls.

Why should followers of Christ be concerned about serving the broader community? Why should churches include community service as part of their mission and vision? Aren't we supposed to "set our minds on things above, not on things on the earth?" (Just kidding!)

Talking Point: Why *should* followers of Christ be concerned about serving the needs of the broader community?

Matthew 5:16, quoted above, is sufficient justification for serving the community. But in addition, consider what God said to Israel after they were taken captive to Babylon, as recorded in Jeremiah 27: 4-7:

Thus says the Lord of hosts, the God of Israel, to all who were carried away captive, whom I have caused to be carried away from Jerusalem to

Babylon: Build houses and dwell in them; plant gardens and eat their fruit. Take wives and beget sons and daughters; and take wives for your sons and give your daughters to husbands, so that they may bear sons and daughters — that you may be increased there, and not diminished. And seek the peace of the city where I have caused you to be carried away captive, and pray to the Lord for it; for in its peace you will have peace. [NKJV]

"Seek the peace of the city...for in its peace you will have peace." This is the Lord's wisdom, and I don't think it applied just to ancient Israel in Babylon. One way to "seek the peace of the city" is to find ways to meet the needs of the communities in which we live.

Robert Lewis is the pastor of a large church in Little Rock, Arkansas. In his excellent book, *The Church of Irresistible Influence,* he relates his journey from being primarily focused with how to grow the size of his congregation to focusing on how his congregation could serve his city. He went to city leaders and asked what *they* needed to have done. As a result, Lewis became instrumental in bringing together other churches in the city to jointly serve the needs of Little Rock.*

Lewis's book caught the attention of a church in my area, the First Presbyterian Church of Bellevue. The leadership of this church went to the city to ask how the church might serve the needs of Bellevue. As a result, an annual community service day has come to be established in Bellevue, called *The Day of Jubilee.* By the fourth year, a dozen other churches in town had joined forces, and about 1,500 people worked to clean and repair public schools and make repairs on homes of families in need. The next DVD clip will give you a picture of what I'm talking about.

**DVD Clip #19
The Day of Jubilee in Bellevue
Approx. 1.5 minutes**

---

* *See also:* The Externally Focused Church *by Rick Rusaw and Eric Swanson.*

If your community doesn't have a church-based, outward-focused community service day, perhaps your church can get one going.

Talking Point: Do the churches in your area have a reputation as "servers of the city?" Why or why not?

Another very effective way of serving the community is when for-profit businesses join forces with non-profit organizations to provide volunteer community labor. Many business leaders would like to help meet the needs of their communities but don't know where to begin. It's relatively easy to write a check to a community assistance fund, and that's a wonderful thing to do. But another way is to rally workers from within companies themselves to provide hands-on time and labor for community service, in addition to writing the check.

Where I live, there is a very effective organization that links business skills, talents and resources with the social, economic and spiritual needs of the city by cooperating with established non-profit organizations that have proven track records. This coordinating organization is called *Liberty Road Foundation*, directed by Dr. John Dammarell.

The roots of *Liberty Road Foundation* go back to 2004, when one company, Liberty Financial Group, Inc., a full-service mortgage company, cooperated with a Seattle-based non-profit organization, *Agros International,* to rebuild a village in Guatemala, called Batzchocolá.

The mortgage company took some of its employees to Guatemala to assist with the labor, and in the process the company recognized the positive effects this experience had on its employees.

Barry Horn, CEO of Liberty Financial Group, reasoned that if the project of rebuilding a village in Guatemala could have such a positive effect on his employees, then community projects in his local area could have similar positive effects on other companies. Thus *Liberty Road Foundation* was founded.

By the end of its first year, twelve businesses in our area were committed to the fourth wheel of work. Thirty-three businesses and individuals had committed to making monthly financial contributions to help support LRF, and sixty volunteers had donated over 700 hours of community service. The next DVD clip will give you a better picture.

DVD Clip #20
Liberty Road Foundation
Approx. 1.5 minutes

Businesses, families and churches working with an "outward focus" can not only function locally, but globally as well. One organization assisting in the global effort is *Agros International,* mentioned above.

Agros works to help businesses and churches labor alongside developing communities in Central America. The next DVD clip will give you a taste of what this organizaiton does in assisting people in developing countries to discover God's pleasure at work.

DVD Clip #21
Agros International
Approx. 4 minutes

The idea of business being a vehicle for missional purposes is generally called "Business As Mission." In the next chapter, we'll take a closer look at the Business As Mission movement.

Talking Point: If anyone in your group has had personal experience working with a company that is committed to benefitting the community (local or global), please share your experience with the group.

Chapter Twelve

Business As Mission

Imagine you've been given the task of bringing a forest to maturity. You've not been given any time-limit, and you have unlimited resources.

You have at least two options. You could plant some seedlings, and then wait, and wait some more. And if all went well, after years and years of growth, and plants pushing roots down deep in the soil and stretching branches toward the sky, you'd have a forest.

The second option? Well, you could dig a bunch of holes and use helicopters to fly hundreds of grown trees into place. Of course this option would save years, but would the result be the same? Imagine what would happen if a major windstorm blew in the day your forest was complete. The second option, while it might look like a forest, wouldn't have the roots it needed, and would likely end up a mass of jumbled logs.

The wisdom of the first option would be quite clear. In this chapter, we'll look at a way of approaching business that will create the kind of environment that will withstand windstorms and truly fulfill and advance the purposes of God in the earth. It's a movement that is following the wisdom of building over time, and driving roots down deep. The movement is called, "Business As Mission."

HISTORY-MAKERS

From the deserts of 7th Century Arabia to the cities of America, Islam now claims 1/5th of the world's population. Currently, this equates to about 1.2 billion people, or 20% of the world's population. In comparison, there are about 1.9 billion people who claim to be Christians.

The country that has the largest population of Muslims in the world is Indonesia, a country thousands of miles from the birthplace of Islam in Saudi Arabia.

Over 200 million Indonesians now claim to be adherents of Islam. That's about 86% of the population. What's noteworthy about all this is that Islam did not become prominent in Indonesia through efforts of Islamic clergy or missionaries. Nor through militant Jihad. It happened through business and trade, over a long period of time.

Michael Baer, the author of *Business As Mission*, tells of an Indonesian Christian whom he once asked why the country had become so predominately Muslim: "She said that when the Western Christians came, primarily from Holland, they built missionary compounds and missionary churches and expected the Indonesian people to come to them. The Muslims, on the other hand, came as traders, farmers, merchants, and businesspeople and simply lived among the natives."

This is a very telling statement. It ought to give every Christian cause to pause and think about how followers of Christ can approach their daily work in a way that will shape the history of nations.

Today, the Islamization of sub-Sahara Africa is taking place in a way similar to how it happened in Indonesia: through business and trade. A pastor friend of mine, Aila Tasse, is very familiar with this process. Aila was born in Ethiopia, and today he plants Christian churches among Muslim communities in northern Kenya and Southern Ethiopia.

Aila was a Muslim himself until age 13. He was brought up in a strong Muslim home, and his father was a leader in the local mosque. When his family discovered Aila had converted to Christianity, through the influence of a Christian schoolteacher, they disowned him, and turned him out of the house. Years later, happily, his parents came to embrace the message of the Gospel, and they became Christians, too.

I met Aila in Indonesia a few years ago, while we were both taking an on-site course through Bakke Graduate University on the culture and history of that country. One of the things we looked at was the interface between Islam and Christianity in that part of the world.

In conversations with Aila in Indonesia, he shared his personal experience with Muslims in Africa. What he shared caused me to be all the more diligent about helping Christians to comprehend how the *way* they approach their daily work can affect the very course of history, not only in America, but around the world.

When I returned home to Seattle, following my trip to Indonesia, I called Aila on the telephone so I could record him for the benefit of all who go through the *God's Pleasure At Work* curriculum. I wanted others to hear what Aila had to say first hand, in his own words. My recording of Aila is contained in the next DVD clip.

DVD Clip #22
Islam in Africa
Approx. 2.5 minutes

When Aila says at the end of the recording, *"...so that's also a challenge,"* he's making a grand understatement. The root problem Aila describes is a problem of Christians embracing a very dualistic view of life while the Muslims have a comprehensive, holistic, view. Muslims do not embrace dualism. But most Christians do. In fact, Western dualism is distasteful to most Muslims. It should be equally distasteful to Christians.

The businesses that Muslims start in Aila's part of the world are not fronts for evangelism. They are very real businesses that meet very real community needs. In the process of meeting the real needs of the community, they invite customers and those they get to know through their businesses into their homes for Koran study. These are people they have built relationships with by providing good daily commerce.

Aila informed me that the African Muslims become respected contributing members of the community, and take seats on the town council. So when the time comes to build a Mosque, it is built in the center of town.

When the Christian missionaries came to Africa, most of them did not make it a priority to help Africans start businesses, or get involved in civil responsibilities.

But we can't point fingers at missionaries! They came to Africa and taught what they had learned at home. The fact of the matter is, a dualistic mindset among Christians is pandemic, not just on the mission field, but at home as well. How often do we hear believers in our own churches speak of having "secular jobs" and others talk of being in "full-time Christian service?"

Dualism, as we discussed at length earlier, has very deep and stubborn roots, going back nearly 2,500 years to the ancient Greeks. It's part of our Western culture. But that doesn't mean we have to hang on to it. The consequences of hanging on to it are particularly serious today. Our future may depend on rising above it.

Talking Point: Why may our future depend on rising above the pull of Western dualism? Is this too strong of a statement?

Dr. Darrell Furgason, a Christian expert in Islam, summarizes the problem this way: "In places like Africa and Indonesia, the church has been intellectually crippled, with one hand tied behind its back. Western missionaries generally brought the Gospel in the way they learned it, as a purely soul-saving faith, with no real bearing on anything else—religion was a mostly personal matter, nothing to do with things like politics, science, law, economics….African people were given the Gospel, but not taught how to build a righteous nation, how to apply Christianity to everything….Muslims see their faith as all-encompassing…"

Notice Dr. Furgason says this is the way the missionaries *generally* brought the Gospel. One notable exception was David Livingstone, the famous Scottish missionary. In a speech at Cambridge, given in 1857, Livingstone declared: "A prospect is now before us of opening Africa for commerce and the Gospel. Providence has been preparing the way…Those two pioneers of civilization—Christianity and commerce—should ever be inseparable; and Englishmen should be warned by the fruits of neglecting that principle…"

Talking Point: Why do you suppose David Livingstone felt that Christianity and commerce "should ever be inseparable?" What biblical justification do you think he would give for this statement?

Regrettably, it wasn't just the Englishmen who neglected this principle. But it is not too late for followers of Christ to make a course adjustment—not only for Africa, but everywhere else as well, both at home and abroad.

The Business As Mission movement is a positive step in that much-needed course adjustment. Michael Baer, in *Business As Mission*, writes: "We are living in the Business Age...Companies, and not countries, will have the greatest impact in our world in the future. Shouldn't the Christian business community see this as a great opportunity? Shouldn't we seek to capitalize on the doors that are open before us? Shouldn't we view this as the ultimate chance for business to play a role in societal transformation and in the spread of the gospel?"

Talking Point: *Should* **we take the position that Baer suggests? If so, what exactly does this mean?**

The Business As Mission movement is about creating legitimate business enterprises that truly serve the needs of communities, and at the same time provide natural opportunities for every-day demonstrations of what a comprehensive Christian worldview looks like when it is "incarnated" through real people with real faith, expressed in the real world of commerce, trade and service. It is a worldview that relates as much to the *temporal* world as it does to the *eternal* world — because these two worlds are intertwined, and *both* are equally God's world!

The previous paragraph is worth reading twice. It summarizes the basic thrust of the GPAW curriculum.

Dr. Al Erisman, co-founder of the *Center for Integrity in Business* at Seattle Pacific University, has some important things to say about Business As Mission in the next DVD clip. Listen carefully.

DVD Clip #23
Dr. Al Erisman on Business As Mission
Approx. 3 minutes

What Al Erisman is describing is a very non-dualistic view of work. It is a comprehensive view that sees work as the natural, normal way to advance the purposes of God in the earth, which, bear in mind, is *His* world.

As Dr. Erisman said, business as mission can be done in *any* kind of work. In fact, *all* business done by followers of Christ should be done as part of the mission and purpose of God for human beings on the great Blue Planet. *Any* legitimate form of work can be an expression of the work of God. *God does His work through carpenters, cops and CEO's!*

FOUR REASONS FOR WORK IN THE TEMPORAL WORLD

The **first** good reason for work in the here-and-now is *to distribute goods and services throughout God's world for the benefit of all people and communities.*

Is it important to God that milk gets to kitchen tables? Is it important to God that furnaces are manufactured so people can stay warm in the winter? Is it important to God that good books are printed so people can learn important things? I think so. Legitimate businesses and services truly benefit people. Illegitimate business and services do not benefit people. If you are involved in a business or service that does not truly benefit people, it is going to be hard, if not impossible, to experience God's pleasure at work.

One of the best books ever written on the topic of work from a biblical perspective is *Your Work Matters To God*, by Doug Sherman and William Hendricks. It is a classic in the field. These astute men define "legitimate" work as "work that somehow contributes to what God wants done in the world, not to what He does not want done." They also say, "If we want to love God through our work *[and, I would add, if we want to experience God's pleasure at work]*, then we need to determine that what we are doing in our jobs is something God wants done, and that we are doing it because God wants it done."

Yes, the distribution of goods and services for the benefit of people is something *God wants done.* When we do this, and do it well, we're actually doing *the work of the Lord.*

Yet businesses do more than distribute goods and services. Have you ever stopped to consider that without healthy businesses, our families, churches and government wouldn't be able to function? Business is the engine that pulls the train on which every other institution rides. I'll say it again: *Business is the engine that pulls the train on which every other institution rides.*

If you recall from Chapter 1, you heard a small portion of a phone conversation I had with Bonnie Wurtzbacher, Vice President of Global Accounts for the Coca-Cola Company, in which she said, "we don't *get* meaning *from* our work, we *bring* meaning *to* our work." I'd like to come back to this phone conversation and have you hear more insights from Bonnie, particularly as she describes the critical role business plays with respect to the functioning of every other institution.

DVD Clip #24
Bonnie Wurzbacher on The Role of Business
Approx. 2 minutes

This leads to the **second** good reason for work in the here-and-now: *to provide the means by which individuals, families, churches, governments and non-profit organizations can function.*

Along these lines, let me say there are many reasons why churches should encourage business people within the congregation. Without business, church doors won't stay open, and communities don't function. Without businesses in the world, there would be no income, and it doesn't take a rocket scientist to understand there would be no offerings to collect. In spite of this fact, instruction on the biblical view of work and the applications of faith in the business world are not often focused priorities for churches, nor for Christian schools.

During the field-testing of GPAW, I taught this course for several groups of Christian businessmen in my area. In surveying them during the course, I discovered that 83% of them had never taken a course on the subject of the integration of biblical worldview with the workplace. Yet virtually all of these men attended church.

I think a deeply ingrained dualistic view of Christianity is at the root of the problem.

I once interviewed twenty pastors in the Seattle area and asked what their level of satisfaction was with how their churches were equipping their congregants to influence the Monday-through-Friday workplace. The average level of satisfaction (on a scale of 1-10, with 10 being the highest) was 4.58. At the same time, twenty out of twenty (100%) believed the local church *should* lay a role in shaping or influencing the Monday-through-Friday workplace. Yet only one pastor indicated that classes on how to apply Christianity to specific aspects of the workplace had *ever* been taught in his church.

Clearly there is a disconnect here. This is a situation that can change, however, with some focused attention.

Talking Point: Why do you think many pastors believe the church should play a role in shaping or influencing the Monday-through-Friday workplace but so few churches offer specific instructions on how to apply Christianity to particular aspects of work?

The **third** reason for work in the temporal world is: *to co-create with God in developing new and meaningful inventions such as the laser pinter, linoleum and symphonies.*

Yes, God has invited us to join Him in an on-going process of creation in the material world. As Gary Starkweather reminded us, God is pleased to have us participate with Him in that on-going process. This is where researchers, artists and innovators can thrive.

The **fourth** reason for work is: *to bring hope, healing, learning and justice to a broken world through endeavors such as feeding the hungry, providing education, civil service and the work of local churches.* This is where pastors, missionaries, workers with non-profit organizations, civil servants and educators can pull their weight. Of course, there is much overlap between these four basic reasons for work, and they are not tight compartments unto themselves.

Talking Point: Which of the four basic reasons for work is the primary focus of *your* work?

What is the most important idea you will take away from this chapter? What is the most important idea you will take away from this book?

Next Steps

Now that you have completed *God's Pleasure At Work: Bridging the Sacred-Secular Divide*, I encourage you to take a small group through this curriculum yourself. Gather together a few co-workers who will meet once a week during the lunch break, or invite a few friends to join you for coffee on Saturday morning at your favorite *latte* spot. You will receive much more out of this curriculum by leading others through it.

If this curriculum has touched you, it will touch others, too. And if we are going to see a difference in the way our culture approaches work, it will require a change of thinking at the grassroots level, with many participants playing their respective parts. *You can play a direct role in this process of cultural transformation by taking a few others through this material.*

If you are a pastor or a teacher, consider teaching the GPAW course as a live-presentation using the same PowerPoint slides, video clips and complete speaking notes I use when presenting this material to groups in live workshops. The live presentation format can provide an outstanding Sunday morning series, or an excellent college, seminary or Christian school course. Contact Worldview Matters at info@worldviewmatters.com for information about this option.

Churches, seminaries, colleges and Christian day-schools must help the Body of Christ to understand the theology of work. The GPAW materials were created for this purpose.

In *GPAW: Bridging the Sacred-Secular Divide*, we have focused on the fourth part of the biblical worldview story, namely, *Restoration.* In the next book in this series, *God's Pleasure At Work: The Difference One Life Can Make,* we will focus on the other three parts of the biblical worldview: *Creation, Fall* and *Redemption.*

As in *Bridging the Sacred-Secular Divide,* there are twelve short chapters in *The Difference One Life Can Make,* with an accompanying DVD. The specific chapter topics are as follows:

1. *The Big Picture:* This chapter deals with three important truths relating to the biblical view of God and Creation, and shows how these truths can affect our approach to work.

2. *Made in the Image of God:* In this chapter, Max DePree, former CEO of the Herman Miller Company, helps us see how the biblical view of Humanity has shaped his company's interaction with employees.

3. What Drives Modern Thought?: For followers of Christ to effectively relate to co-workers, clients and customers in postmodern times, it helps to understand how we got to this stage in history. This chapter provides a clear backdrop for understanding what postmodernism is about.

4. The 20th Century Turn: In this chapter, we will examine three characteristics of postmodern thought that affect the way many customers, clients and employees approach morality and ethics today.

5. The Upside of Postmodern Times: Postmodernism has an upside and a downside. This chapter reveals aspects of both sides, and how the upside can open doors for followers of Christ to be a spiritual influence at work.

6. Spiritual Influence At Work: This chapter continues to focus on how to be a spiritual influence in today's workplace. The example of Don Flow, CEO of Flow Automotive, is celebrated.

7. Responding Rightly When Things Go Wrongly: When we focus on "doing the right thing," we are actually focusing on the wrong thing! To focus on *loving the Lord* rather than on "being good" is to put the emphasis where it needs to be.

8. The Difference One Life Can Make: At one time or another, we are all faced with the challenge of doing the right thing when it isn't appreciated by others in the workplace. The inspirational example of Jack vanHartesvelt is celebrated in this chapter.

9. "But I'm just a hairdresser!": What exactly is the "work of the Lord?" Does it include hairdressing? This chapter presents "a theology for homemakers, nurses and doctors, plumbers, stockbrokers, politicians and farmers," as seen through the keen eyes of Paul Stevens, author of *The Other Six Days.*

10. What in the World is the Kingdom of God?: What does the Kingdom of God actually look like? What does it mean to "actualize" the Kingdom of God in our daily lives? How we view the Kingdom of God has a lot to do with how we view our work in the here-and-now.

11. The Biblical Worldview Finder: The "Biblical Worldview Finder," explained in this chapter, is a "thought prompter" that helps followers of Christ to get perspective on workplace problems and challenges.

12. Vital Friends and Parting Thoughts: Followers of Christ in the workplace are wise to incorporate the assistance of "Vital Friends," and to have a "Personal Board of Directors" for counsel. In this chapter, you'll find out why and how.

I look forward to continuing the GPAW journey with you! But for now, please give a listening ear to some important concluding remarks and pastoral advice from Dr. Lowell Bakke, Professor of Pastoral Studies at Bakke Graduate University, who was a pastor for 35 years.

DVD Clip #25
Concluding Remarks and Advice from Dr. Lowell Bakke
Approx. 3 minutes

Talking Point: Would you feel comfortable going to your pastor or priest to discuss what Lowell Bakke has suggested? Why or why not?

Afterword

Life's Greatest Question

by John D. Beckett

For some time I had been thinking about writing a small booklet for business and professional people that would present a clear, compact summary of the Gospel. But I had put off the assignment—deeming it "important," not "urgent."

That changed on February 1, 2003. A call from a business colleague alerted me to an unfolding disaster in our nation's space program. "Turn on the TV," Jim urged.

I was shocked by what I saw. The Columbia space shuttle, returning to earth from a 16-day mission, was breaking up. Luminous fragments streaked like a shower of comets across a clear blue Texas sky. The elegant spacecraft was just fifteen minutes from touching down at Cape Canaveral.

Soon, broadcasters flashed pictures of the astronauts—six Americans and one Israeli. In an instant those seven were facing eternity. I was gripped with the question: "Did they know the Lord?"

I turned off the TV, went to my study, and began writing the message I had, for too long, put off. My challenge was to present the familiar "good news" of the Gospel in a way that wasn't bound by clichés or religious jargon. It had to be thorough, fully supported by Scripture, approachable, yet simple.

Eventually a booklet was published under the title *Coming Home.* While it had a remarkable reach, its impact moved to a dramatic new level almost exactly three years after the Columbia disaster. That is when, at the suggestion of the CEO of an Internet savvy ministry in California, the message went on the Internet as *www.lifesgreatestquestion.com.*

To help people find the site, we began buying ads on Google

and Yahoo. To our amazement, we found people visiting in droves from every corner of the world — and to our *utter* amazement, discovered that one in eight told us they had decided to become a follower of Christ!

We found the more we advertised the more people came, with no indication of saturation. With uncanny predictability, one in eight said "yes" to surrendering their lives to Christ. We learned we could track terms by which people were searching and found the dominant search topic was "the meaning of life."

We have now expanded into websites in several additional languages in the belief that no one should have to learn another language to be able to understand the Gospel. We have developed a 30-day study guide to help stabilize new believers. We are experimenting with other Internet-friendly means to accelerate the growth of these fresh converts.

Frankly, we don't know where this will lead. What we *do* know is that we can affordably reach over one million visitors each year — each initiating a search on his or her personal schedule and terms. We believe the Holy Spirit is prompting these searches, and we stand amazed that one in eight will decide to follow Christ.

Who would have imagined that the Internet — in many ways a very dark place — would be used to reach hungry hearts throughout the world? God is truly moving, as the prophets said would happen, to cover the earth with the knowledge of the Lord as the waters cover the sea.

The first step in knowing God's pleasure at work is to come to know God Himself. Personally. It is a step of faith each one of us must take, and we can only take it by ourselves.

But we do not take it alone.

If you have never seriously considered this vital first step, I invite you to visit me at *www.lifesgreatestquestion.com*.

Appendix
50 Biblical Premises Relating To Work*

Biblical Worldview Truths That Relate to
GOD and Work

God is present everywhere in my workplace. [Ps. 139:8 Where can I go from Your Spirit? Or where can I flee from Your presence? If I ascend into heaven, You are there; If I make my bed in hell, behold, You are there.]

God knows all my thoughts and my co-workers thoughts, and is fully aware of the details of each life connected with my work. [Luke 12:6-7 Are not five sparrows sold for two farthings, and not one of them is forgotten before God? But even the very hairs of your head are all numbered.]

God desires a personal relationship with me and with all of my co-workers and customers. [I Tim. 2:4 God desires all men to be saved and to come to the knowledge of the truth.]

God communicates with me on the job, and He will give me wisdom when I ask. [II Tim. 3:16-17 All Scripture is given by inspiration of God, and is profitable for doctrine, for reproof, for correction, for instruction in righteousness that the man of God may be perfect, thoroughly furnished unto all good works; John 16:13 …when He, the Spirit of Truth is come, He will guide you into all truth…]

God is all-powerful, and there is no problem I face at work that is too difficult for Him. [Jer. 32:17 Ah, Lord God! Behold, You have made the heavens and the earth by Your great power and outstretched arm. There is nothing too hard for You.]

God is righteous and cares about justice being done throughout every aspect of my work. [Ps. 33:5 He loves righteousness and justice…]

**Biblical truths outlined in this section have been adapted from biblical truth statements developed by The Biblical Worldview Institute, www.biblicalworldviewinstitute. Used by permission.*

God is merciful and forgives. [I John 1:9 If we confess our sins, He is faithful and just to forgive us our sins and to cleanse us from all unrighteousness.]

God has given people great diversity of gifts and abilities which He desires to be freely exercised for the benefit of all involved in the workplace. [James 1:17 Every good gift and every perfect gift is from above…; Eph. 2:10 For we are His workmanship, created in Christ Jesus for good works, which God prepared beforehand that we should walk in them…]

God answers prayer on the job as well as off. [Luke 11:9-11 So I say to you, ask, and it will be given to you; seek, and you will find; knock, and it will be opened to you.]

God works through redeemed people to accomplish His purposes in the workplace. [Matt. 5:16 Let your light so shine before men, that they may see your good works and glorify your Father in heaven.]

Biblical Worldview Truths That Relate to CREATION and Work

My entire workplace and everything in it was spoken into existence by the Creator's willing choice. [John. 1:3 All things were made through Him, and without Him nothing was made that was made.]

All material things in my workplace are continually sustained by God. [Col. 1:17 All things were created through Him and for Him. And He is before all things, and in Him all things consist (hold together).]

God's created things in my workplace include both physical and spiritual realities. [Col. 1:16 For by Him all things were created that are in heaven and that are on earth, visible and invisible, whether thrones or dominions or principalities or powers.]

God's created things in my workplace include both temporal and eternal realities. [II Cor. 4:18 For the things which are seen are temporary, but the things which are not seen are eternal. Col. 1:16-17 All things were created through Him and for Him.]

All aspects of God's creation in my workplace speak of His power and authority over all. [Rom 1:20 For since the creation of the world His invisible attributes are clearly seen, being understood by the things that are made, even His eternal power and Godhead…]

My workplace is affected by corruption due to humanity's sin. [Rom. 5:12 Therefore, just as through one man sin entered the world, and death through sin, and thus death spread to all men, because all sinned.]

My workplace and everything in it has not been forsaken by God, in spite of the Fall. [Gen. 3:21 (after the Fall) …for Adam and his wife the Lord God made tunics of skin, and clothed them; John 3:17 For God did not send His Son into the world to condemn the world, but that the world through Him might be saved.]

My workplace and everything in it remains God's own possession, and therefore everything in my workplace has great significance. [Ps. 24:1 The earth is the Lord's and all it contains.]

My workplace is a realm that God intends for me to responsibly steward and govern. [Ps. 8:4-8 You have made [mankind] to have dominion over the works of Your hands; You have put all things under his feet, all sheep and oxen—even the beasts of the field, the birds of the air, and the fish of the sea that pass through the paths of the seas.]

Spiritual forces exist that oppose God and His work in my workplace. [Eph. 6:11-12 Put on the whole armor of God, that you may be able to stand against the wiles of the devil. For we do not wrestle against flesh and blood, but against principalities, against powers, against the rulers of the darkness of this age, against spiritual hosts of wickedness in the heavenly places.]

Biblical Worldview Truths That Relate to HUMANITY and Work

My co-workers and customers are all created in the likeness and image of God, and possess intrinsic value and inherent worth on this basis. [Gen. 1:26-28 Then God said, "Let Us make man in Our image, according to Our likeness…"; See also Gen. 9:6.]

Every co-worker is a spiritual as well as a physical being, having both physical and spiritual needs. [Gen. 2:7 And the Lord God formed man of the dust of the ground, and breathed into his nostrils the breath of life; and man became a living being; Deut. 6:5 You shall love the Lord your God with all your heart, with all your soul, and with all your strength.]

I and all my co-workers and customers have been born with a basic nature that tends to go its own way rather than God's way. [Isa. 53:6 All we like sheep have gone astray; We have turned, every one, to his own way…; Rom. 3:23 For all have sinned and fall short of the glory of God.]

Human pain, suffering, sorrow, and alienation from God are the results of sin's effects, and none of my co-workers or customers are exempt from these realities. [Rom. 5:12 …by one man sin entered into the world, and death by sin; and so death passed upon all men…]

My customers and co-workers can be restored to a right relationship with God through trust in the finished work of Christ. [John 3:14-15 …as Moses lifted up the serpent in the wilderness, even so must the Son of Man be lifted up, that whoever believes in Him should not perish but have eternal life.]

Since I am a believer in Christ, I have the Holy Spirit dwelling within me and He empowers me to live a God-honoring life in the workplace. [I John. 4:4 He who is in you is greater than he who is in the world.]

I can model what it means to be a dedicated follower of Christ by observing His commands in the context of my daily work. [Matt. 28:19-20 Go therefore and make disciples of all the nations…teaching them to observe all things that I have commanded you…]

As a Christ-follower, I am to be ready to give a reason for the hope that is within me to any co-worker or customer who asks. [I Pet. 3:15 …always be ready to give a defense to everyone who asks you a reason for the hope that is in you…]

I, and my co-workers, have been endowed by God with special gifts and abilities for ruling over the material world, and when these talents are put to good use in the workplace, the result is increased joyful service in the age to come. [Matt. 25:21 "…you were faithful over a few things, I will make you ruler over many things. Enter into the joy of your lord."]

All my co-workers and customers will experience physical death followed by eternal fellowship with God or eternal separation from Him. [Matt. 25:32-34; 41 All the nations will be gathered before Him, and He will separate them one from another…Then the King will say to those on His right hand, "Come, you blessed of My Father, inherit the kingdom prepared for you from the foundation of the world"…Then He will also say to those on the left hand, "Depart from Me, you cursed, into the everlasting fire prepared for the devil and his angels…'"]

Biblical Worldview Truths That Relate to
MORAL ORDER and Work

The two foremost workplace responsibilities I have are to love the Lord with all my heart, mind and strength, and to love my co-workers and customers as myself. [Matt. 22:36-40 Jesus said to him, "You shall love the Lord your God with all your heart, with all your soul, and with all your mind….You shall love your neighbor as yourself."]

I am responsible to God and ultimately accountable to God for all my workplace actions. [Heb. 9:27 …it is appointed for men to die once, but after this the judgment…]

Ultimately, all legitimate moral order is determined by God, not by my boss, the Board of Directors, or my customers. [Ex. 20:1-3 "…You shall have no other gods before Me…"]

The Bible is God's divinely inspired gift, and His authoritative rule of faith and conduct for the workplace. [II Tim. 3:16-17 All Scripture is given by inspiration of God, and is profitable for doctrine, for reproof, for correction, for instruction in righteousness, that the man of God may be complete, thoroughly equipped for every good work.]

The non-optional and non-negotiable moral order of God applies to every aspect of my work. [Deut. 10:12 What does the Lord your God require of you, but to fear the Lord your God, to walk in all His ways and to love Him, to serve the Lord your God with all your heart and with all your soul, and with all your strength.]

Genuine freedom is the internal self-control that comes from self-government under God, through the enablement of the Holy Spirit — regardless of my circumstances at work. [Gal. 5:1-23 …do not be entangled again with a yoke of bondage…you who attempt to be justified by law; you have fallen from grace…I say then: Walk in the Spirit, and you shall not fulfill the lust of the flesh…But the fruit of the Spirit is love, joy, peace, longsuffering, kindness, goodness, faithfulness, gentleness, self-control…]

To obey God in all things related to my work-life is the most intelligent thing I can do. [Ps. 119:97-99 Oh, how I love Your law! It is my meditation all the day. You, through Your commandments, make me wiser than my enemies; For they are ever with me. I have more understanding than all my teachers…]

Since the Fall, human beings (including myself and every co-worker and customer I come in contact with) have experienced an internal problem with sin – a natural "bent" to go our own way rather than God's way, and to be a law unto ourselves. [Isa. 53:6 All we like sheep have gone astray; we have turned, every one, to his own way…]

Although I have the God-given ability to break His moral laws on the job, I do not have the right to break them. [Matt. 4:10 You shall worship the Lord your God, and Him only you shall serve.]

Violation of God's moral order at work results in pain – for the violator and for others. [Rom. 5:12 …by one man sin entered into the world, and death by sin; and so death passed upon all men… See also Ex. 20, Deut. 28, Psalm 119, Matt. 5-7 and Romans 6.]

Biblical Worldview Truths That Relate to PURPOSE and Work

The First Commission God gave to mankind was to rule over all the earth – and that space includes my workplace. [Gen. 1:26-28 Then God said, "Let Us make man in Our image, according to Our likeness; let them rule…over all the earth…"]

God desires His will to be done in my workplace as it is in heaven. [Luke 11:2 So Jesus said to them, "Our Father in heaven…Your kingdom come. Your will be done on earth as it is in heaven…"]

My function as a believer in Christ is to "salt" and "light" the workplace. [Matt. 5:13-16 You are the salt of the earth…You are the light of the world…Let your light so shine before men, that they may see your good works and glorify your Father in heaven.]

The real purpose of all the things I work with is found in Christ's purpose for all things. [Rev. 4:11 …Thou hast created all things, and for Thy pleasure they are and were created.]

There is a purpose for myself as well as for each co-worker and customer I know. [II Pet. 3:9 The Lord is...not willing that any should perish but that all should come to repentance. Eph. 2:10 For we are his workmanship, created in Christ Jesus unto good works...]

The Bible helps me to understand God's plan and purpose for my work. [II Tim. 3:16-17 All Scripture is given by inspiration of God, and is profitable for doctrine, for reproof, for correction, for instruction in righteousness, that the man of God may be complete, thoroughly equipped for every good work.]

God gives me daily opportunities in the workplace to serve others in the name of Christ. [Matt.5:16 Let your light so shine before men, that they may see your good works and glorify your Father in heaven.]

God's good purpose for civil government relates to my workplace. [Rom. 13:1-4 For there is no authority except from God, and the authorities that exist are appointed by God...For rulers are not a terror to good works, but to evil...For he is God's minister to you for good.]

Christ's Great Commission to "make disciples" can be done in the context of the workplace. [Matt. 28:18-20 Go ye therefore, and teach all nations, baptizing them in the name of the Father, and of the Son, and of the Holy Ghost: Teaching them to observe all things whatsoever I have commanded you...]

By God's grace, He will work through redeemed people to bring His light to every sphere of work. [Matt. 5:13-16 You are the salt of the earth...You are the light of the world. A city that is set on a hill cannot be hidden. Nor do they light a lamp and put it under a basket, but on a lampstand, and it gives light to all who are in the house. Let your light so shine before men, that they may see your good works and glorify your Father in heaven.]

Use this Order Form or Call Toll-Free 877.624.0230

qty. ___ *Assumptions That Affect Our Lives* @ $16 each: ________

(for information on the DVD curriculum *Think Again!*, based on the
Assumptions That Affect Our Lives book, call the number above)

God's Pleasure At Work:

<u>Volume 1</u>: Bridging the Sacred-Secular Divide

<u>Volume 2</u>: The Difference One Life Can Make

<u>*CIRCLE the volume you wish to purchase above; indicate quantity below:*</u>

qty. ___ 1-Person Study (1 DVD + 1 text) @ $39 each: ________

___ 5-Person Study (1 DVD + 5 texts) @ $99 each: ________

___ 10-Person Study (1 DVD + 10 texts) @ $169 each: ________

___ 20-Person Study (1 DVD + 20 texts) @ $299 each: ________

___ Additional Text(s) @ $15 each: ________

___ Additional DVD(s) @ $30 each: ________

Shipping and Handling (add 10%): ________

WA residents add sales tax at your local rate: ________

TOTAL: ________

Name: ____

Phone: _______________E-mail: ______________________________

Shipping Address: ____

Apt/Suite: _______City/State: ___________________________Zip: ________

*Send this Order Form with money order or check to Worldview Matters, 2800 122nd
Place NE, Bellevue, WA 98005. If using a credit card (below), fax this form to
509.275.5817*

Please charge this to my: **VISA MC** (circle one)

Credit Card Number: _______________________________________

Expiration Date: ___________________________

Security Code (on back of card): ________

Name and address on card, if different from name and shipping
address above: _______________________________________